Edward J. Carter is currently the parish priest at St Peter's Didcot in Oxford Diocese, as well as being Area Dean of the Wallingford Deanery. He has degrees in economics and theology, and completed some postgraduate studies in Christian ethics at Oxford University in 2006. He teaches part of the ethics programme at Ripon College, Cuddesdon, with a particular focus on the use of the Bible as a guide to Christian living. Edward is married to Sarah and they have two teenage sons.

D1627913

Text copyright © Edward J. Carter and Jo Fageant 2010
Illustrations copyright © Edward J. Carter 2010
The author asserts the moral right
to be identified as the author of this work

Published by
The Bible Reading Fellowship
15 The Chambers, Vineyard
Abingdon OX14 3FE
United Kingdom
Tel: +44 (0)1865 319700
Email: enquiries@brf.org.uk
Website: www.brf.org.uk
BRF is a registered charity

ISBN 978 1 84101 699 3

First published 2010
10 9 8 7 6 5 4 3 2 1 0

Acknowledgments
Unless otherwise stated, scripture quotations are taken from the Contemporary English
Version of the Bible published by HarperCollins Publishers, copyright © 1991, 1992, 1995
American Bible Society.

A catalogue record for this book is available from the British Library

Printed in Singapore by Craft Print International Ltd

Story Assemblies
for the School Year

36 ready-to-use assemblies with five-minute stories, teacher's notes and RE follow-up

Edward J Carter

Ideas for classroom follow-up by Jo Fageant

Dedicated to the children of Northbourne School
in Didcot, who heard these stories when they
were first being told.

Comments from people who have used the prototype material

[God's Storyteller] has proved to be very effective and lively.

I found the school staff and children very enthusiastic… There has been real engagement.

[Re: Felix's garden] We have an autistic child who engaged with collective worship last week for the first time and said to me in the afternoon, 'The ribbons came off.'

There was a distinct 'oh' when I told the school it was the end of the story today.

The children have been very engaged with the storyline and were often eager to know the next part of the story rather than wait a week—the cliff-hanger endings work well. The simple props have been great, just enough to give the children a focus and link the story elements together.

We are loving it!

The materials are great, easy to use and very comprehensive.

One of our children has now got a [God's Storyteller] notebook, where she jots down her thoughts, pictures and prayers.

Children had excellent recall of the story and we used the follow-up in class assemblies.

The staff have really enjoyed using the linking material and found it very useful.

Endorsements

Story Assemblies for the School Year has radically altered our delivery of assemblies for both whole-school and class-based assemblies. Our new and improved assemblies start with the delivery of a story to the whole school on Monday, staff included. On Tuesday class assemblies focus on the 'I wonder...' aspect, as I leave that part out of the story. This allows class teachers to interpret this aspect at the correct cognitive level for their year groups, and gives the teacher time to draw out that thinking process of 'I wonder...'. On Wednesday and Thursday assemblies, we focus on the 'Value'. Then on Fridays, teachers and visiting lay preachers tell the Bible story or explore the symbolism to round off the week. It's really exciting that our vicar and lay preacher have been equally excited about supporting *Story Assemblies for the School Year* in their delivery of assembly too.

The biggest impact has been on the children. They love the stories and even though they know there is always a 'cliff-hanger' at the end of each weekly assembly, there is still an audible groan when it ends!

Mrs Christina Moss
Head teacher, The Queen Anne Royal Free CE First School, Windsor

This book really will be an answer to all your assembly needs. Main celebrations of the Christian year are skilfully included and, as the year unfolds, links between the six stories emerge. Schools piloting this resource have been so thrilled that they are hungry for more! Having visited almost all of the schools using these assembly stories, I have seen children and staff excited, enthused and engaged. These are not just the stories of a children's entertainer; the impact goes deeper—children are invited to reflect upon the big questions of life, with the spiritual and moral dimension coming to the fore as, week by week, term by term, the material retells the story of God's love.

Julie Mintern
Schools Adviser, Oxford Diocesan Board of Education

Preface

Children love stories, and I've really enjoyed telling the stories in this book when leading assemblies. I wanted to keep my assemblies broadly Christian by telling the big story of God's love for the world, but I've tried to make it fun by helping the children imagine themselves as part of the story as well. It encourages them to think about their own values and behaviour, not by learning the right answers to give but by making a leap of imagination and identifying themselves with the characters in the stories.

My stories are in the tradition of great Christian storytellers such as C.S. Lewis and his *Narnia Chronicles*, but designed for school assemblies. Jesus taught using parables and, in a similar way, the stories in this book are essentially parables about God and the events in the Bible. If you use them all, they take you through the whole school year. I'm delighted to be sharing them with you.

Edward Carter

Contents

Section Five: Jesus: risen and ascended...............144

Values: Peace and understanding

Story: The amazing flowerpot

Section Six: Paul's journeys...177

Values: Responsibility and tolerance

Story: The vital race

Templates

*

Foreword

The Christian faith was a set of stories before it was a set of statements; and where the statements can sometimes seem cold and difficult to understand, the stories are warm and inviting. Jesus himself taught in stories and puzzles and riddles. In order to understand his stories, you had to enter into them. Indeed, the whole Bible can be understood as the story of God's love—or, should we say, a great library of stories—in which the purposes of God are unfolded to the world; but, again, unfolded in such a way that we are invited to enter in. In this sense the story is always unfinished. God wants us to be part of it.

At its best, the church carries on this tradition of telling stories and inviting people to respond. We get to the statements of our faith *through* the stories. They enshrine and protect our doctrine. They also mean that the message can never get separated from the messenger. It is therefore vitally important that children are introduced to the grand sweep of the biblical narrative—and all the stories that it contains. As they enter into the story, they receive the riches of the Christian faith. They become part of the story themselves.

Edward Carter is a priest, a theologian and a brilliant storyteller. This rich collection of *Story Assemblies for the School Year* introduces children to Felix's garden, Cassandra's crown, an amazing flowerpot and much else besides—and, through them, to God the storyteller, who has a treasured place within the story of his love for each of us.

The material has been field-tested in Edward's parish and in quite a number of church schools in the diocese of Oxford. I have every confidence that it will prove to be an entertaining, instructive and illuminating resource. After all, everyone loves a good story, and this book offers new angles on the greatest story of all.

+*Stephen Cottrell, Bishop of Reading*

*

Introduction

There are many ways you could use the material in this book, but it has been designed so that the main story episodes are told once a week. At the end of each set of six episodes, there is a final celebration, which connects to a seasonal theme such as Christmas or Easter.

Before the first assembly you will need to:

- Choose someone (or several people to take it in turns) to be the storyteller.
- Make the storyteller's prop for the story in question, using the instructions.
- Quickly run through the first story episode so that it is familiar.

Extra things that you could do to increase the impact of the stories include:

- Make a badge for the storyteller to wear (if you wish, the wording on the badge could be 'God's Storyteller'; see sample on page 210).
- Make a display board on which children's work, connected to the stories, can be displayed.
- Choose suitable music to be played before and after the assembly.
- Choose a song to sing at the assembly, which links to the story episode.
- Use your classroom-based follow-up time to connect to the stories.
- Keep the teaching staff informed about the stories and advise them about good curriculum links.

Suggestions are given throughout the book on how the above ideas can best be put into practice.

There are two ways of telling the stories. You can either read them in full from this book, as you would from any book you are using for a story. Alternatively, you can tell the story without a script, using notes as prompts. The storyteller's prop helps to illustrate the story and acts as a good prompt in itself. A notes card for each episode is available to download from the Barnabas website, www.barnabasinschools.org.uk/schools6993. You can also download the key Bible verse card for each story from this website.

Although the material in this book has been designed for use in school assemblies, it can also be used as the basis for an RE course focused on Christianity.

Year outline

Story Assemblies for the School Year includes material for one school year. The year is divided into six sections, corresponding to six blocks of teaching time.

Section One: God's creation
Values: Beauty and appreciation
Story: Felix's garden
Key Bible verse: 'God looked at what he had done, and it was good' (Genesis 1:12)
Concluding celebration: Harvest thanksgiving

Section Two: The prophets
Values: Patience and trust
Story: The candle-maker
Key Bible verse: 'Someone more powerful is going to come' (Mark 1:7)
Concluding celebration: Christmas

Section Three: The discipleship parables
Values: Love and honesty

Story: Cassandra's crown
Key Bible verse: 'Jesus said, "I have explained the secrets about the kingdom of heaven to you"' (Matthew 13:11)
Concluding celebration: Christingle or Pancake Day

Section Four: The humility of Jesus
Values: Humility and hope
Story: The witness birds
Key Bible verse: 'Christ was humble. He obeyed God and even died on a cross' (Philippians 2:8)
Concluding celebration: Holy Week or Easter

Section Five: Jesus: risen and ascended
Values: Peace and understanding
Story: The amazing flowerpot
Key Bible verse: 'A seed must die before it can sprout from the ground' (1 Corinthians 15:36)
Concluding celebration: Pentecost

Section Six: Paul's journeys
Values: Responsibility and tolerance
Story: The vital race
Key Bible verse: 'I run towards the goal, so that I can win the prize of being called to heaven' (Philippians 3:14)
Concluding celebration: Leavers' farewell

Key to songs

TCH: *The Children's Hymn Book* (Kevin Mayhew, 1997)
JP: *Junior Praise* (Marshall Pickering, 1986)
SoF: *Songs of Fellowship* (Combined) (Kingsway Music, 1991)
HO&N: *Hymns Old & New* (Kevin Mayhew, 1996)

*

Section One

God's creation

Key Bible verse

God looked at what he had done, and it was good.
GENESIS 1:12

Values

Beauty and appreciation

This section is designed to run from the start of the school year in September through to the October break. The theme is God's creation and, in the big story of God's love for the world, we are at the beginning—when the goodness of what God has made is spoilt by human selfishness. When we imagine ourselves within this part of the story, we learn to appreciate the care that has gone into making a beautiful world and we experience sadness when that beauty is damaged.

The story of Felix's garden is told in six parts and illustrates the biblical account of the creation, the story of disobedience and the covenant between God and Noah. It is found in Genesis 1—9.

- Week One: Genesis 1:1–10 and 14–19
- Week Two: Genesis 1:11–12 and 20–25
- Week Three: Genesis 1:26–31
- Week Four: Genesis 3:1–7
- Week Five: Genesis 3:14–19
- Week Six: Genesis 6:1—9:17

The storyteller's prop consists of a wooden pole and seven coloured ribbons. The wooden pole can be about 80cm long, of the type used for a garden rake. The ribbons should each be about 100cm long. You will need one each of the following colours: red, orange, yellow, green, blue, dark purple (indigo) and light purple (violet). A photograph of an example prop can be found on the website, www.barnabasinschools.org.uk/schools6993.

Suggested music

Suggestions for pre-recorded music that could be used at the start and end of assemblies include:

- 'All things bright and beautiful' (John Rutter, Collegium, CSCD515)
- 'For the beauty of the earth' (John Rutter, Collegium, CSCD515)
- 'Morning mood' from *Peer Gynt Suite* (Edvard Grieg, Naxos 8.570236)
- 'Winter' from *The Four Seasons* (Vivaldi, Naxos 8.571071) (at the end of Week 4, both beginning and end of Week 5, and beginning of Week 6)

Suggestions for songs that could be sung at assemblies include:

- All things bright and beautiful (JP 6)
- Be still, for the presence of the Lord (SoF 40)
- Father, I place into your hands (JP 42)
- He's got the whole wide world in his hands (JP 78)
- If I were a butterfly (JP 94)
- Morning has broken (JP 166)
- Our God is so great (TCH 169)
- Rise and shine (Week Six) (JP 210)
- Think of a world without any flowers (Week Five) (JP 254)

*

Felix's garden: Week One

Bible link

This week's Bible passage link is Genesis 1:1–10, 14–19, which recounts the way in which God set out the basic patterns in the universe that make life possible. These include light, water, earth, and the passage of days and seasons.

Key theme

This week's key theme is 'preparation'. This is a major element of the first episode of 'Felix's garden'. The idea of preparation, along with appreciation and beauty, can feature throughout any and all of the worship and curriculum links this week—for example, the importance of thinking and finding out before we act, preparation and patience needed in making a garden, gathering information and organising it into a presentation for a meeting of the school council, preparation of art materials and so on. In general, there is an understanding that being prepared usually makes projects work better. Preparation is an important idea connected with harvest, which will be celebrated by many schools during this term—for example, preparing land to grow crops (short- and long-term), preparation and rehearsal for harvest service/celebration and so on.

Episode One

I wonder if any of you have been away on holiday over the summer. Did any of you help with the packing before you went? If you did help, you'll know that going on holiday takes lots of preparation. You have to book your tickets and arrange a place to stay. You have to pack your clothes and your toothbrush, and your passport if you're going to another country. Without good preparations, you couldn't enjoy your holiday.

Today I want to start telling you a story about someone who had to make good preparations. It's a very special story, because it tells us about God.

Once upon a time, there was a little boy called Felix, who loved running around outside and playing in the fresh air. But one day, when he was playing in a rough old patch of ground where there was absolutely nothing growing, he had a brilliant idea. He decided that he would try to turn the empty space into a garden—his own garden! In fact, he decided to try to make it the most beautiful garden in the whole world.

Felix knew he would have to make lots of preparations if the rough, empty space was to be transformed into a beautiful garden. He knew he would have to put all his skill into it.

Felix started work the very next day. He took a big spade and he kept digging and digging. The earth was a beautiful rich red colour, and soon he could see the garden beginning to appear. It took all his skill to do that digging. Once he'd done enough digging, he stopped and enjoyed looking at his work.

Felix could see that he needed to mark out some flower beds and vegetable beds if it was going to be a proper garden. So he fetched some wood that he knew he could use, and he carefully made some fence posts, bits of fence and some wooden edges for the beds. It took all his skill to make those things from the wood. When he had finished, he used them all to mark out the different parts of the garden. Now he could really see the garden taking shape, and he stopped to enjoy looking at his work.

Just then, the sun came out and shone brightly. The whole

garden looked so beautiful in the sunlight. Felix looked at all that he'd done and he was very pleased. It was so beautiful that he wanted to do something to celebrate his new garden. So he took a wooden pole, like this one *(show the pole)* … and he stuck it into the ground in the middle of his garden. Then he took a fine red ribbon and he tied it carefully on to the pole. *(Attach the red ribbon to the pole.)* 'That will remind me of the rich red earth in my garden,' he said to himself. Then he took a fine orange ribbon and he tied it on to the pole. *(Attach the orange ribbon to the pole.)* 'That will remind me of the wooden fences and borders that mark out my garden,' he said to himself. Then he took a fine yellow ribbon and he tied it on to the pole with the other two. *(Attach the yellow ribbon to the pole.)* 'That will remind me of the lovely sunshine that fills my garden,' he said to himself.

At just that moment, a little gust of wind came and blew through Felix's garden. The three ribbons fluttered in the wind. *(Wave the pole so that the ribbons fly out.)* It was a beautiful sight and Felix laughed with delight. It really was a very beautiful garden. But just then he had a wonderful idea…

I haven't got time now to tell you what Felix's idea was, but I promise to carry on with my story next week. It's a very special story, because it reminds us about God and how he prepares everything that exists in the world, including the sun and the earth. God makes sure that everything is well ordered, so it's the perfect place for life.

Just like Felix, who prepared his garden so carefully using all his skill, God created the world and all that is in it using all his love. Felix was so pleased with his garden that he put a pole with beautiful ribbons in the middle of it. *(Wave the pole so that the ribbons fly out.)* He laughed with delight.

In the Bible, right at the start in the book of Genesis, it says, 'God looked at what he had done, and it was good.' Just like Felix, God is so delighted with his creation. Maybe this pole and its ribbons can remind us of that. Maybe we could try to remember what the different ribbons mean.

Wouldn't it have been great to have been like Felix and begin making a garden? I wonder what it would have felt like to prepare everything so carefully—all that hard work! I wonder if we'd have put a pole with ribbons in our garden. Would we have laughed with delight when we saw the ribbons flying in the wind? *(Wave the pole so that the ribbons fly out.)* And I wonder what God must have felt like when he saw the beauty of what he'd made. I wonder.

Suggested prayer

Lord God, thank you for the story of Felix and his beautiful garden, and thank you for the beauty of your creation. You made heaven and earth and all that is in them and, when you looked at what you had made, you saw that it was good. Help us to remember how much you love this world, and help us to care for it, too. Amen

*

Felix's garden: Week Two

Bible link

This week's Bible passage link is Genesis 1:11–12, 20–25, which recounts the way in which God gives life to a great variety of plants and animals.

Key theme

This week's key theme is 'growing'. Successful growing depends on good preparation. Alongside growing go ideas about change and patience. Curriculum links could explore how and why vegetables are good foods, with discussion about children's favourite vegetables and flowers. Vegetarian and other diets could also be investigated. It would be good to study how different foods and flowers grow in different parts of the world and climates, and how vegetables are used in various ways in other cultures.

Episode Two

I wonder if any of you remember the story that we began hearing last week. Who can remember the name of the boy and what he was starting to make? And do you remember this? *(Produce the pole with the three ribbons and wave it around.)* What do the three ribbons mean?

I hope you remember as well that this story about Felix's garden reminds us of God and everything that he's made. Just like Felix, who prepared his garden very carefully using all his skill, so God created the world and all that is in it using all his love.

Felix had just had a really good idea for his beautiful garden to make it even more amazing, and a big smile came over his face. He ran quickly to an old shed that was nearby and went inside. It was a bit gloomy but he could just see piles of old pots and plastic trays and different garden tools. He began hunting around carefully in the dark.

Suddenly he found the thing he was looking for. Hidden at the back, down in one corner, was a small sack. Felix picked it up carefully and took it outside. It was tied at the top with a piece of string but he untied the knot very easily and looked into the sack. It was full of seeds and bulbs. Every kind of seed and bulb was in that sack!

Felix put his hand into the sack, grabbed a handful of seeds and scattered them gently in one part of his garden that he'd marked out with the wooden edges. Straight away, little green shoots started pushing up through the rich red earth, helped by the strong sunshine. They were lovely carrots—Felix's favourite vegetable—and when he pulled one up it was a beautiful orange colour, all fat and juicy!

When Felix had finished scattering all the seeds from the sack in his garden, there were green shoots springing up everywhere. His garden was full of life! And there weren't just vegetables. There were beautiful flowers as well—dandelions, daisies, buttercups, roses—every kind of flower.

Felix walked around his garden, enjoying everything he could see. He remembered that his favourite flower was the bluebell, and he started hunting for one. Suddenly he found one in a corner of his garden, just by the fence, growing strongly in the rich red earth, lovely and blue in the sunshine. Felix was so pleased! He laughed with delight!

Just then, Felix noticed the pole with the ribbons blowing in the wind. *(Wave the pole so that the ribbons fly out.)* He wanted to celebrate all the plants and flowers that were growing in his garden, so he decided to tie two more ribbons on to the pole. First he took a fine green ribbon and he tied it carefully on to the pole with the others. *(Attach the green ribbon to the pole.)* 'That will remind me of all the green plants and vegetables in my garden,' he said to himself. Then he took a fine blue ribbon and he tied it on to the pole. *(Attach the blue ribbon to the pole.)* 'That will remind me of all the flowers in my garden, especially my favourite, the bluebell,' he said to himself.

At just that moment, a little gust of wind came and blew through Felix's garden. The five ribbons fluttered in the wind. *(Wave the pole so that the ribbons fly out.)* It was a beautiful sight and Felix laughed with delight. It really was a very beautiful garden, full of so many things. But as he looked around, Felix knew that it wasn't quite finished yet. He needed something more to complete his beautiful garden...

Next week I'll tell you some more of my story, and I hope we'll find out what Felix still needed in his garden to make it complete. But it's a very special story, because it reminds us about God and how he fills creation with all kinds of life—not just vegetables and plants but animals as well. There are living things of every size and colour and shape, and God gives them all life.

Just like Felix, who filled his garden with so many plants and flowers using the seeds and bulbs from that old sack, so God has filled the world with so many living things using all his love. Felix was so pleased with his garden that he put a pole with beautiful ribbons in the middle of it. *(Wave the pole so that the ribbons fly out.)* He laughed with delight. In the Bible, right at the start in the book of Genesis, it says, 'God looked at what he had done, and it was good.' Just like Felix, God is delighted with his creation. This pole and its ribbons can remind us of that.

Wouldn't it have been great to have been like Felix and make a garden? I wonder what it would have felt like to scatter those seeds and see them all spring up. I wonder if we'd have put a pole with ribbons in our garden. Would we have laughed with delight when we saw the ribbons flying in the wind? And I wonder what God must have felt like when he saw the beauty of what he'd made, and all the different living things. I wonder.

Suggested prayer

Lord God, thank you for the story of Felix and his beautiful garden, and thank you for the beauty of your creation, full of every living plant and creature. You made heaven and earth and all that is in them and, when you looked at what you had made, you saw that it was good. Help us to remember how much you love this world, and help us to care for it, too. Amen

Felix's garden: Week Three

Bible link

This week's Bible passage link is Genesis 1:26–31, which recounts the way in which human beings have been set over creation, to use it and care for it.

Key theme

This week's key theme is 'stewardship'. The meaning of stewardship can be explored together with the way the skills, understandings and talents of each individual can be used to care for the environment.

Episode Three

I wonder if any of you remember the story that we've been hearing. Who can remember the name of the boy and what he is making? And do you remember this? (Produce the pole with the five ribbons and wave it around.) What do the five ribbons mean?

I hope you remember as well that this story about Felix's garden reminds us of God and everything that he's made. Just like Felix, who filled his garden with so many plants, God fills the world with every kind of living plant and creature, using all his love.

Felix knew that his garden still wasn't quite complete. Suddenly he realised what he needed to do! He ran back to the old shed and went inside again. It was still very gloomy but soon he found what he wanted. It was a little net full of delicious nuts. Quickly he ran back to his garden and hung the net of nuts up from one of the fence posts. Then he sat down in one corner of his garden and waited to see what would happen.

Suddenly there was a flash of colour. A little robin was flying towards the bag of nuts and soon it was pecking away, enjoying the food. Then the robin flew down from the bag of nuts and landed on one of the paths in the garden. There were some untidy sticks lying there but the robin picked them up and took them away. Felix smiled as he watched what was happening. 'The robin is tidying up my garden,' he said to himself. Then the robin flew down to one place in the garden where the plants were all very close together and tangled up. He started untangling the leaves and making everything neat. Felix began laughing quietly to himself. 'That robin is a bit bossy but he's making my garden really tidy. In fact, he's caring for everything that's here. I'm so pleased he's arrived.'

Just then, the robin flew over to the pole with the ribbons. They'd got a bit twisted up in the wind, but the robin started untwisting them. *(Shake the pole so that the ribbons fly out.)* That gave Felix an idea. He decided to add two more ribbons to the pole. First of all, he took a purple ribbon and tied it carefully on to the pole with the others. *(Attach the purple ribbon to the pole.)* 'This colour is what kings wear, and it will remind me of how the bossy robin is like a king in my garden,' he said to himself. Then he took a violet ribbon and he tied it on to the pole. *(Attach the violet ribbon to the pole.)* 'This is such a gentle and caring colour, and it will remind me of how the robin cares for everything in the garden, keeping it so tidy,' he said to himself.

At just that moment, a little gust of wind came and blew through Felix's garden. The seven ribbons fluttered in the wind. *(Wave the pole so that the ribbons fly out.)* It was a beautiful sight and Felix laughed with delight. It really was a very beautiful garden, full of so many things. Felix looked around and saw how good everything was. But then he remembered one last thing that the garden needed…

Next week I'll tell you some more, and perhaps we'll find out the very last thing that Felix needed in his garden. It's a very special story, because it reminds us about God, and it reminds us about human beings as well. You see, human beings are a bit like kings over creation. We make fields to grow food, and nets to catch fish. God has given us the freedom to build houses and roads, cars and aeroplanes. We rule over nature like kings. But God has put us on earth to care for creation as well. Human beings can protect delicate plants and animals and the whole environment. The bossy robin, who was like a king in Felix's garden but cared for it as well, reminds us of human beings.

Just like Felix, who brought a robin into his garden, using the nuts in the net, so God has put human beings in the world, using all his love. Felix was so pleased with his garden that he put a pole with beautiful ribbons in the middle of it. *(Wave the pole so that the ribbons fly out.)* He laughed with delight. In the Bible, right at the start in the book of Genesis, it says, 'God looked at what he had done, and it was good.' Just like Felix, God is delighted with his creation. This pole and its ribbons can remind us of that.

Wouldn't it have been great to have been like Felix and make a garden? I wonder what it would have felt like to hang up that net of nuts and see the robin arrive. I wonder if we'd have put a pole with ribbons in our garden to celebrate. Would we have laughed with delight when we saw the ribbons flying in the wind? *(Wave the pole so that the ribbons fly out.)* And I wonder what

God must have felt like when he saw the beauty of what he'd made, all the living things and the people as well. I wonder.

Suggested prayer

Lord God, thank you for the story of Felix and his beautiful garden, and thank you for the beauty of your creation, full of every living plant and creature, and with people as well. You made heaven and earth and all that is in them and, when you looked at what you had made, you saw that it was good. Help us to remember how much you love this world, and help us to care for it, too. Amen

Felix's garden: Week Four

Bible link

This week's Bible passage link is Genesis 3:1–7, which recounts the way in which human beings first disobeyed God.

Key theme

This week's key theme is 'water', which builds on the theme of stewardship. The importance of water is clear in this part of the story. Thirst and drought, together with the work of charities that help to bring clean water to parts of the world where people have not had it, make rich areas of exploration. The destructive power of flooding is illustrated at the end of Episode Four of the story, and this idea continues into the fifth week.

Alternative themes could be the importance of rules, and pollution. These ideas could be carried over into thoughts about rights and responsibilities in Week Five.

Episode Four

I wonder if any of you remember the story that we've been hearing. Who can remember the name of the boy and what he is making? And do you remember this? (*Produce the pole with the seven ribbons and wave it around.*) What do the seven ribbons mean?

I hope you remember as well that this story about Felix's garden reminds us of God and everything that he's made. Just like Felix, who prepared his garden so carefully, filled it with so many plants and brought the robin there, so God fills the world with every kind of living plant and creature, and people as well, using all his love.

Felix realised that he needed one last thing to make his garden complete. He needed a supply of water to make sure it was the most beautiful garden ever made. 'Water will help the plants to grow and will make sure my garden lasts for ever,' thought Felix to himself.

So Felix ran to the old shed one more time. This time, though, instead of going in, he looked around the back. There he found a big water butt which could hold lots and lots of water. He carried it carefully back to his garden and he set it up on some big stones right in the middle, next to the pole with the ribbons. Then he filled it with water, right to the top, so that everything was ready. It was a very big water butt and it only just balanced on the stones, but Felix was so pleased. His garden was perfect!

Felix looked around at everything he could see—the rich red earth, the strong fences and wooden edges to the beds, the shining sun, the green plants, the flowers (especially his favourite, the bluebell) and, of course, the little robin busily flying around keeping the garden tidy. In the middle, the ribbons on the pole fluttered in the wind. *(Wave the pole so that the ribbons fly out.)* Felix stretched out his arms and gave a big yawn. All that work had made him very tired and he needed a sleep. So he called the little robin over and told him not to go near the water butt. 'Look, there are plenty of delicious nuts left and you'll be busy caring for my garden,' said Felix to the robin. 'But you mustn't go near the water butt, because it's very deep and it could be dangerous.'

Felix lay down just by the gate and in no time at all he was fast asleep, having a lovely rest. The sun was still shining and the breeze blowing. The robin came over to see if Felix really was asleep. Then he flew right round the garden until he came to the pole with the ribbons, and he landed on top of the pole. The water butt was right next to the pole, and the robin really wanted to see into the water butt, even though Felix had told him not to go near. He leaned out as far as he could but he couldn't see properly, so he hopped off the top of the pole and perched on the edge of the water butt. Then he tried to lean down to reach the water, which was dark and deep, but he couldn't reach far enough. So he picked up a stick from the garden in his beak, and came back to perch on the water butt again. He poked the stick down as hard as he could to try to get to the water.

Suddenly everything seemed to be moving! The water butt was rocking backwards and forwards! Then it crashed over and knocked the pole down... *(push all the ribbons swiftly off the pole into the air and throw the pole noisily down to the floor)* ... and all the seven ribbons went flying. Water was everywhere and all the plants were ruined. And the robin had completely disappeared...

Next week I'll tell you some more of the story, and maybe we'll find out what became of the robin and of Felix's garden. My story is a very special story, because it reminds us about God and his creation. You see, God has made such a beautiful world but something has happened to spoil it. Bad things happen. People get hurt. There's pollution, and the beautiful world we live in is often ruined. In the Bible we can read the story of Adam and Eve. They ate fruit from a special tree, even though God had told them not to. They were just like the robin, who

31

disobeyed Felix and tipped the water butt over. Felix's garden has been spoilt, just as the world has been spoilt by greedy and thoughtless people.

Right at the start in the book of Genesis, it says, 'God looked at what he had done, and it was good.' But what does it feel like to say those words now? Felix's beautiful garden is ruined. The pole with the seven different ribbons has been knocked over.

It would have been great to have been Felix and make a garden, but I wonder what it would have felt like, after all that work, to have everything ruined. And I wonder what God must have felt like when he saw human beings spoil the good creation that he'd made. I wonder.

Suggested prayer

Lord God, thank you for the story of Felix and his beautiful garden, and thank you for the beauty of your creation. You made everything so well but now we have spoilt it, so that people fight and argue and nature is often ruined. Help us to remember how much you love this world, and help us to care for it, too. Amen

Felix's garden: Week Five

Bible link

This week's Bible passage link is Genesis 3:14–19, which recounts the way in which human disobedience led to pain and suffering.

Key theme

This week's key theme is 'rights and responsibilities' or 'consequences'. Everything we do and say has an impact on other people around us. Rules are provided for the good of all, and disobedience can have unpleasant consequences. This part of the story also enables an exploration of feelings of guilt and repentance. Links could be made with school rewards and sanctions.

Episode Five

(The pole and the first five ribbons are lying scattered on the floor at the front and the storyteller seems not to have noticed.)

Shush! Felix is asleep! He's dreaming!

In his dream, Felix could see everything in his perfect garden, which he'd worked so hard to make. He could see the rich red earth. He could see the strong fences and the wooden edges of the flower beds. The sun was shining brightly on all the lovely green plants and vegetables—and, of course, there was his favourite flower of all, the bluebell. There was the lovely robin, so kind and helpful, flying around. And in the middle, next to the water butt, was the pole with its seven beautiful ribbons.

I'm sure you remember as well that this story about Felix's garden reminds us of God and everything that he's made. Just like Felix, who prepared his garden so carefully, filled it with so many plants and brought the robin there, so God fills the world with every kind of living plant and creature, and people as well.

Shush, shush! Felix is asleep and dreaming!

But then Felix stretched out his arms and rubbed his eyes, and he was awake. He stood up and looked around. Something seemed to be wrong. Where was the pole with the ribbons? Where were all his lovely plants and flowers? He walked around the garden and his feet splashed in the water. Everything was ruined. All his hard work had been spoilt.

Then Felix found the red ribbon floating in the water. He picked it up and it dripped with water. (*Pick up the crumpled red ribbon.*) Who can remember what this ribbon reminds us of? But now the rich red earth was under water. Felix splashed on his way and he found the orange ribbon. (*Pick up the crumpled orange ribbon.*) Who can remember what it reminds us of? But now all the pieces of wood had been pushed over. Then Felix found the yellow ribbon. (*Pick up the crumpled yellow ribbon.*) Who can remember what it reminds us of? But now a cloud had blocked out the sunshine. Then Felix found the green ribbon. (*Pick up the crumpled green ribbon.*) Who can remember what it reminds us of? But now all the lovely green plants were drowning in water. And then Felix found the blue ribbon. (*Pick up the crumpled blue ribbon.*) Who can remember what it reminds us of? But now his favourite bluebells were all waterlogged and ruined.

Felix was feeling angry. His garden had been wrecked. He kept searching in his garden with a frown on his face and found the wooden pole, but he couldn't find the last two ribbons anywhere—the purple and violet ones. He couldn't see the little robin anywhere, either.

Felix was worried about the robin, so he called out, 'Robin! Little robin! Where are you? I can't see you!' But there was no answer. Then Felix noticed the empty water butt, lying on a muddy patch of ground. He saw little footprints on the top of the water butt and he realised they belonged to the robin. Then Felix shouted with an angry voice, 'Robin! Where are you?' Still there was no answer. Felix peered into the dark water butt. He could just see something hiding down at the very bottom. It was the robin, with the last two wet ribbons hanging from his beak.

'What have you done?' said Felix sternly to the robin, but the robin kept silent. 'You've ruined my beautiful garden and everything is spoilt. It will be much harder now for you to find food. It won't be a nice place to live any more, in my garden. And I won't be able to trust you any more, either.' But the robin just listened. 'I made you like a king in this garden. That's why I used the purple ribbon. And once upon a time you cared for this garden. That's why I used the violet ribbon. Haven't you got anything to say for yourself?'

The little robin started to open his beak. Then very quietly he whispered a question to Felix: 'Do you still love me…?'

Next week I'll tell you some more of the story, and maybe we'll find out what Felix's answer was. As you know, my story of Felix's garden is a very special story, because it reminds us about God and his creation. You see, God has made such a beautiful world, but when it was spoilt it made life much harder. We have to work hard when we'd rather be playing or resting. We end up arguing with other people and sometimes nasty things happen to us. In the Bible we can read about Adam and Eve and how their lives became much harder after they disobeyed God, just like the robin in Felix's garden, who will find life in the garden much tougher now.

It would have been great to have been Felix and make a garden, but I wonder what it would have felt like to splash through all the water and see everything ruined. I wonder what it would have felt like to talk to the robin, who'd spoilt everything. And I wonder what God must have felt like when he saw human beings spoil the good creation that he'd made. I wonder what God wanted to say then. I wonder.

Suggested prayer

Lord God, thank you for the story of Felix and his beautiful garden, and thank you for the beauty of your creation. You made everything so well, but now we have spoilt it and our lives are often filled with sadness and trouble. Help us to remember how much you love this world, and help us to care for it, too. Amen

Felix's garden: Week Six

Bible link

This week's Bible passage link is Genesis 6:1—9:17, especially 9:8–17. This recounts the way in which God set a rainbow in the sky to mark a new beginning for human beings.

Key theme

This week's key theme is 'new beginnings and forgiveness'. This last part of the story provides a happy ending. The robin is forgiven for his disobedience and pupils will be able to empathise with his relief at being forgiven and loved by Felix, having been given the opportunity for a fresh start.

Episode Six

(The storyteller starts by holding the empty pole. The ribbons should be linked together in a chain and crumpled in a ball.)

I wonder if any of you remember the story we've been hearing. And do you remember the wooden pole? What do the seven ribbons mean? Oh! There are no ribbons! What's happened?

I hope you remember as well that this story about Felix's garden reminds us of God and his creation. The robin disobeyed Felix and now his life will be much harder. Felix won't be able to trust him. It's the same for human beings, who have disobeyed God and have to work hard just to survive.

But wait! The robin has asked Felix a question: 'Do you still love me…?'

Felix crouched there, looking into the water butt, at the robin. His face looked sad and angry. Then he took the ribbons that had been soaked by the water and tried to put them back on to the pole, but he couldn't attach them properly. *(Pretend to attach the ribbons to the end of the pole, then let them fall to the floor.)*

Then he started talking to the robin. His voice became angrier as he kept on speaking. 'To start with, there was nothing here at all,' he said. 'I prepared this garden all by myself. I dug the rich red earth; that was why I tied a red ribbon to the pole. I marked out all the edges and borders with pieces of wood; that was why I used an orange ribbon. The sun shone and everything was perfect, so I used a yellow ribbon. Then I planted seeds and saw beautiful plants and flowers grow up in my garden, so I tied a green ribbon and a blue ribbon to the pole as well.

'Then I put nuts here and you came to my garden. I asked you to look after it very carefully and I trusted you. Of all the things in my beautiful garden, you were the most special. You even had two ribbons, a purple one and a violet one, to remind me that you were like a king in my garden and to show how much you cared for it. But you didn't listen to me. You disobeyed me. You tipped the water butt over and ruined my garden! And now you ask me, "Do you still love me…?"'

Felix stopped talking. Gradually his angry face changed. He smiled and said, 'Of course I still love you!' Then he jumped up and waved the pole in the air, and the robin was amazed to see that all the ribbons had been joined together. *(Attach the chain of ribbons to the pole and wave it in the air.)*

The robin was so excited. He flew out of the water butt and high into the sky, and then round and round the garden. 'Felix does still love me,' he was saying to himself again and again.

Then the robin noticed that the sun was shining again and the water had almost all drained away. The earth was still rich and red, and the plants were still alive. Felix was saying, 'I love you so much, we can make a new beginning.' He was waving the rainbow ribbons in the sky, and the robin knew that he was the happiest he'd ever been.

That's almost the end of my story about Felix and his garden. As you know, this story tells us about God and his creation. The robin had disobeyed Felix, just as human beings disobey God and spoil this beautiful world. But the amazing thing is that God still loves us, just as Felix still loved the robin even though he'd done such a bad thing.

The rainbow ribbons were a sign of Felix's love. I wonder if any of you remember about a rainbow in the Bible? In the Bible, it tells us how a great flood covered the earth, but one man and his family built a big boat, an ark, so that they would be safe. The man was called Noah and, when the flood ended, Noah was safe again because God still loved him. As a sign of God's love, a rainbow appeared in the sky above. That rainbow wasn't just for Noah. It was a sign that God still loved his creation, just the same as when he'd first made it. Do you remember what it says right at the start of the book of Genesis? Yes, that's right, 'God looked at what he had done, and it was good.'

Wouldn't it have been great to have been like Felix and made a garden? How would we have made our garden special, I wonder? Which plants would have been our favourites? Would we have put nuts out to see if a little robin would eat them? And if a robin had ruined our garden, would we have said, 'Of course I still love you'? Would we really have meant it, like Felix did?

I wonder what it must have felt like to be Noah, living in a world full of bad things but knowing that God still loved him and his family. I wonder what it felt like to see that rainbow. I wonder how it changed Noah's life. If we'd been there, I wonder how it would have changed our lives, too. I wonder.

Suggested prayer

Lord God, thank you for the story of Felix and his beautiful garden, and thank you for the beauty of your creation. Even though it's spoilt when people are greedy and don't think about what they're doing, you still love us and you give us the chance of a new beginning. Lord God, help us to remember how much you love this world, and help us to care for it, too. Amen

*

Felix's garden: Concluding celebration

The story of Felix's garden ends very successfully with a harvest thanksgiving, with suitable songs, poems, readings and prayers. You could also organise a collection of food for a local charity or sheltered housing complex. The concluding episode of the story connects to the harvest theme.

Concluding episode

(Wave the pole with the seven ribbons, fixed separately to the pole once again, not as a chain.) Do you remember the story about Felix's garden? What do these seven ribbons mean?

Do you remember as well how this story tells us about the way that God gives life to everything, and how much he loves his creation? He even forgives people who spoil things, when they are sorry.

Felix loved his garden. Every day he enjoyed watching things grow. Most of all, he loved seeing the little robin look after the garden, and, as the months went by, more and more birds came to live there. Before long, the sound of birds chirping and singing filled the whole garden. Felix was delighted. He loved seeing the garden so full of life.

Time passed by and yet more birds came to live in Felix's beautiful garden. It was so full now that sometimes the birds would argue about where they could make their nests. Even though there was lots of food, the birds would squabble. They all wanted the best food for themselves.

By now, Felix had grown much older. In fact, he wasn't a boy any more. He was an elderly man with a long white beard. The garden was very old as well, full of large trees and tall plants, and there were hundreds of birds living there. You couldn't go anywhere without seeing them and hearing the noises they made.

Only one thing in the garden hadn't changed. The wooden pole with its seven brightly coloured ribbons was still there, right in the middle. One day, a tiny robin, who had hatched out of his egg only a few weeks before, landed on the pole and looked at it curiously. The ribbons were very fine but he couldn't understand what they meant. He tried asking the other birds but they were all too busy finding food or arguing with each other. None of them seemed to know why the pole, with its ribbons, was there.

Then the robin noticed an elderly man by the gate. It was Felix, with his long white beard and a weary look on his face. The robin flew over to the gate and asked Felix about the ribbons. A twinkle came into Felix's eye. He was so pleased that the robin was interested in the pole and ribbons. 'I put that pole there, little robin,' said Felix. 'I put it right in the middle of the garden when I first created it.'

The robin was so excited to discover that Felix had actually made the garden! Then Felix started to explain what the ribbons meant. 'The red one is for the lovely rich red earth that I dug. The orange one reminds me of the fences and borders that I made for the flower beds. The yellow one is for the bright sun that made the garden warm. Then the green and blue ribbons are for all the plants and flowers in my garden. And last of all, the purple and the violet ribbons remind me of another little robin, the same as you. He was like a king in my garden but he cared for it as well. He made mistakes but in the end he did his best to help make the garden a lovely place to live in. I even tied all the ribbons together to make a rainbow, so he'd know I would always love him.'

Felix's face was sad again now. 'What's the matter, Sir?' asked the little robin. 'Why are you so sad?' So Felix explained how more and more birds had come to live in the garden. They had forgotten all about the rainbow, and they had forgotten that they were supposed to take care of everything in the garden. They'd become greedy and wouldn't share their food with each other. The weakest birds were scared away and the strongest ones grew rich.

'That's dreadful!' squeaked the little robin. 'Why didn't you tell them to share properly? Why didn't you shout at them and force them to be good?'

'I did try telling them,' said Felix, 'but they never listened to me. In the end, I even turned myself into a bird, and I went into the garden to show them how they should behave. I thought they would listen to me if I was like them, but even then they ignored me. Worse than that, they all attacked me and drove me away.'

By now, the robin was very sad. 'I wish I could help,' he whispered. Felix thought for a minute or two. 'There is one thing you can do,' he said. 'You could go and tell the other birds about the pole and the ribbons. You could tell them about the rainbow. You could tell them the whole story of my garden. If they knew the whole story, they might learn to share things properly again and take care of my garden.'

The little robin chirped excitedly. 'Yes, I will!' he said. 'I'll tell everyone the whole story, so they'll know what the garden is meant to be like.'

We are like that little robin. God wants us to go and tell people how to share the fruits of the earth. God wants us to look after the world and everything in it. God wants us to tell people how much he loves everything he's made.

*

Felix's garden:
Ideas for classroom follow-up

Alongside the main weekly assembly, you can develop the themes of the story in your classroom. One or more of the following ideas could be used.

- Read the story of the creation from the Bible or a storybook retelling—for example, *The Book of Books* by Trevor Dennis (Lion Hudson, 2003), which is written as a poem. This could be accompanied with a PowerPoint presentation of appropriate pictures.
- Explore the creation narrative through a game of pass-the-parcel. Alternate layers of black wrapping paper (to represent night) with brightly coloured paper (to correspond with each part of the creation story). Unwrap keeping time with the storyteller.
- Different year groups could produce a box, or page for a big book, representing different aspects of the creation story. Alternatively, these could be displayed on the storyboard which is used to develop further the themes of collective worship.
- Keeping in time with the storyteller, use mime or drama, dance, music and movement to tell the story.
- Focusing on values of appreciation and beauty, consider the diversity of people and how they appreciate different things. Explore multicultural aspects, what other people look like, where they come from, the diversity of beauty and how we all see beauty differently.
- Consider the beauty of a face, looking at older and younger faces. You might study Mother Teresa's face, for example, representing beauty of a different sort.
- Looking at their own faces, pupils could be encouraged to connect with and appreciate their senses.

- Create, over a week or more, a collage of things that pupils consider to be beautiful. Everyone can contribute something to this project.
- Using the song 'Look at the world' by John Rutter, and others of a similar nature that celebrate the beauty and variety of the world and recognise our responsibility to care for it, pupils could prepare images in PowerPoint to fit with verses or lines of the songs.
- Reflect on ways in which you can make your classroom and school more attractive.
- Think about ways to take a pride in what you do and feel a sense of achievement.

Within the curriculum, you could make links with science, art, geography, literacy, PHSE, Citizenship and RE. You can find ideas on the website, www.barnabasinschools.org.uk/schools6993.

*

The prophets

Key Bible verse

'Someone more powerful is going to come.'
MARK 1:7

Values

Patience and trust

This section is designed to run from after the October break until the Christmas holiday. The theme is the prophets and, in the big story of God's love for the world, we are remembering the people who kept saying that God would one day come and join them. When we imagine ourselves within this part of the story, we learn about the patience and trust needed when we wait for God to do something special for us.

The story of the candle-maker is told in six parts and illustrates the biblical accounts of the message of the prophets as they spoke about the arrival of God's chosen king (the Messiah). These are found mainly in the various Old Testament books of the prophets. The account of John the Baptist is at the start of the New Testament.

- Week One: Stories about Amos and the wickedness of God's people (key verse: Amos 3:10)
- Week Two: The story of Jonah and the need to turn back to God (repent) (key verses: Jonah 3:8b–9)
- Week Three: The story of Hosea and God's loving mercy (key verse: Hosea 14:4)

- Week Four: The story of Ezekiel and God's promise of a new heart (key verse: Ezekiel 36:26)
- Week Five: Stories about Isaiah and clearing a pathway for God (key verse: Isaiah 40:3)
- Week Six: The story of John the Baptist in Mark 1:4–8 (key verse: Mark 1:7)

The storyteller's prop used for the story of the candle-maker consists of a set of seven candles as follows:

- A cracked-effect candle
- A yellow candle
- A silver candle
- A glittery candle
- A strongly scented candle
- A purple candle
- Either a baptism candle or a church paschal candle

You will also need a small candle lighter or a box of matches. You may wish to use a tray on which to place the candles. The candles should be large enough to burn for a couple of hours and still be mostly unconsumed. It is more interesting if they are of different shapes—perhaps square, cylindrical, spherical and so forth. A photograph of an example prop for the story of the candle-maker can be found on the website, www.barnabasinschools.org.uk/schools6993.

Suggested music

Suggestions for pre-recorded music that could be used at the start and end of assemblies include:

- Extracts from *Messiah* (G.F. Handel, Naxos 8.553258)
- 'Hail, gladdening light' (Charles Wood, EMI CDCFP4641)

Suggestions for songs that could be sung at assemblies include:

- All over the world the Spirit is moving (JP 5)
- Hills of the north, rejoice (Weeks Five and Six) (HO&N 209)
- How lovely on the mountains are the feet of him (Weeks Five and Six) (JP 84)
- I, the Lord of sea and sky (TCH 102)
- I'm accepted, I'm forgiven (Week Three) (SoF 229)
- Jubilate (JP 145)
- Make way, make way, for Christ the King (Weeks Five and Six) (SoF 384)
- Spirit of the living God (SoF 511)

The candle-maker: Week One

Bible link

This week's Bible passage link is Amos 3:10, which recounts the wickedness of God's people.

Key theme

This week's key theme is 'right and wrong'. Pupils can be encouraged to consider how we know or decide what is right and wrong and discover sources of authority that help us. Explore ideas about giving in to and resisting temptation, and invite responses to Amos' idea that people don't know how to do right.

Episode One

Today I want to start telling you a new story about a candle-maker. It's a special story because it reminds us about God and the things he's done.

Once upon a time, there was a candle-maker who made candles for all the people in the town. She was very clever at making candles but she was also very lonely. She lived alone in a small house with just a little mouse to keep her company. A long time before, she had had lots of friends but then she moved away to a new town and left them all behind. Her friends had given her a mysterious mirror when she moved. They had told the candle-maker that one day she would hold a candle in front of the mirror, and the mirror would tell her that this candle was the most special and precious candle ever made.

One day, the candle-maker was at home when suddenly there was a knock at the door. Three tall men, all dressed in dark coats and scarves, were on her doorstep. 'We'd like you to make us a candle, please,' they said. 'We need it tonight. It mustn't blow out easily if we take it outside, because we're going to rob the royal palace!' The candle-maker was shocked. The palace was full of gold and silver and jewels. These robbers would be able to steal a fortune if she helped them—but she knew she could make a candle that would be perfect, a special candle that would make a bright light in the dark and not blow out.

The little mouse was rushing around, looking very worried and squeaking, but the candle-maker went and found just the right mould. She melted some dark wax carefully in a pan and poured it into the mould. When it had got cold again, she slowly took it out of the mould. *(Show the cracked candle, and ask one of the children to help light it.)* It was a beautiful candle, but it did seem to have cracks all over it. She took it quickly to the three tall men and they snatched it from her and ran out of the door, still wearing their dark coats and scarves.

It was dark by then and the candle-maker was tired. She sat in her favourite chair and the little mouse came and sat next to her. He was looking quite sad, but the candle-maker was too tired to care, and soon she was fast asleep.

Suddenly she woke up with a start. There was a noise at the door! When she ran to see who was there, all she could find was the cracked candle that she'd made, still alight, on the doorstep. She carried it carefully inside and, as she closed the door, she caught sight of the mysterious mirror hanging in the hallway. 'Maybe this is the most special and precious candle ever made,' she said to herself. 'I must ask the mirror!'

She carried the candle over to the mirror and held it up. After a few moments, the mirror began to speak. 'This is indeed a fine candle, beautifully made, but it doesn't know how to do anything good. It's been used by robbers and you weren't right to make it. This candle is not the most special and precious candle ever made. Another one, much better, is still to come.'

The candle-maker was sad to hear what the mirror had said. She was about to blow the candle out when she heard another noise outside, at the door. It was the little mouse, looking very bedraggled. 'Where have you been?' cried the candle-maker.

I haven't got time to tell you any more of my story today. Maybe next time we'll find out where the mouse had been. It's a very special story that I'm telling, because it reminds us about God and his own people, the Israelites. They were waiting and waiting for a very special person, called the Messiah, to arrive— just as the candle-maker was waiting to see if the candle she held in front of the mirror was the most special and precious one ever made. God's prophets kept telling the Israelites about the Messiah. One of them was the prophet Amos, and he said, 'People don't even know how to do right', because the Israelites had become like the robbers in the story. The greatest of the prophets was called John the Baptist, but even he said, 'Someone more powerful is going to come', just as the mirror told the candle-maker that an even better candle was still to come.

I wonder what it would have been like to have been the candle-maker. It would have been fun making candles, but what about the one she made for the robbers? I wonder how she felt when the mirror said it wasn't the best one, the one she'd been hoping for, but that another one—the best one ever made—was still to come. It must have been exciting thinking about that candle. And I wonder what God's special people, the Israelites, must have felt when the prophet Amos told them that they didn't know how to do right. I wonder if they were excited thinking about the Messiah and when he would arrive. I wonder.

Suggested prayer

Lord God, thank you for candles and the light they make, and thank you for the story of the candle-maker. As we look at this cracked candle, we remember that bad things do happen in the world. Help us to hear the message of the prophets about someone special who was still to come, someone who would shine as the light for the whole world. Amen

The candle-maker: Week Two

Bible link

This week's Bible passage link is Jonah 3:8b–9, which recounts the need to repent (or turn back to God).

Key theme

This week's key theme is 'repentance', exploring what it feels like to be sorry. How easy or difficult can it be to say 'sorry'? Pupils might consider how they respond to people who apologise to them. How should we respond? There are many stories that include this theme—for example, *The Rainbow Fish* by Marcus Pfister (North-South Books, 1998).

Episode Two

(Light the cracked candle.) Do you remember the story we began last week? What was this candle used for? And was it the best candle ever made?

I hope you remember that this story reminds us about the prophets in the Bible. The message the mirror brought, saying that the candle-maker had done a bad thing, is like the message from the prophet Amos, who said, 'People don't know how to do right.' In the Bible, though, the greatest of the prophets was called John the Baptist and he said, 'Someone more powerful is going to come.' I wonder who he meant.

The mouse had just arrived home looking very bedraggled. He'd been out, following the three tall men, and he'd seen them go all the way to the palace, using the light of the cracked candle to guide them. A bit later on, he'd seen them leaving with a big sack that clinked, as though it was full of treasure.

Now that the mouse was home, he started squeaking noisily at the candle-maker. He was very angry with her. She guessed he'd seen the robbers stealing from the palace, and she knew that the men could only have done it with her help, but the mouse was being so annoying. He was starting to give her a headache with his noisy squeaking!

The candle-maker did her best to ignore the little mouse completely, but wherever she went, the mouse followed her, still squeaking away. Then she got so cross with the mouse that she started shouting at him. 'Be quiet, little mouse!' she yelled as loudly as she could, but however loud she shouted, the mouse kept on squeaking noisily.

Finally, she got so furious with the little mouse that she picked him up and threw him right out of the window! 'At last, some peace and quiet,' she said to herself, but after a minute or two she heard the squeaking begin again. The mouse had crawled back into the house through a tiny gap under the door. She just couldn't get rid of him.

The candle-maker saw that the little mouse was scampering around the cracked candle and shaking his head. She remembered what a bad thing she'd done, making the candle for the robbers. A tear started rolling down her cheek and she began to feel very sorry for what she'd done. If only she hadn't made that candle after all. Soon she was crying very hard, yet she could feel the mouse stroking against her.

Suddenly the candle-maker had a good idea. She would make another candle to show how sorry she was. She went and found the perfect mould and melted some yellow wax carefully into a pan. Then she poured it into the mould. When it had got cold again, she slowly took it out of the mould. *(Show the yellow candle, and ask one of the children to help light it.)* It was a beautiful candle and it shone very brightly.

'Maybe this is the most special and precious candle ever made,' she said to herself. 'I must ask the mirror!' So she carried the candle over to the mysterious mirror and waited for it to say something. After a few moments, the mirror began to speak. 'This is indeed a lovely candle, because you made it as a sign that you are sorry for what you did wrong. But this candle is not the most special and precious candle ever made. Another one, even better, is still to come.' The candle-maker was thinking about what the mirror had said when she heard something land on the doormat. 'I wonder what it is,' she said to herself.

I haven't got time to tell you any more of my story today. Maybe next time we'll find out what had just come through the letterbox. It's a very special story that I'm telling, because it reminds us about God and his own people, the Israelites. They were waiting and waiting for a very special person, called the Messiah, just like the candle-maker who was waiting to see if the candle she held in front of the mirror was the most special and precious one ever made. God's prophets kept telling the Israelites about the Messiah. One of them was the prophet Jonah, and he said, 'Pray to the Lord God with all your heart and stop being sinful and cruel', because the people had to turn away from wrong things and turn back to God. The greatest of the prophets was called John the Baptist, but even he said, 'Someone more powerful is going to come', just as the mirror told the candle-maker that an even better candle was still to come.

I wonder what it would have been like, to have been the candle-maker. It would have been fun making candles, and very special to make the yellow candle. I wonder how she felt when the mirror said it wasn't the best one, the one she'd been hoping for, but that another one—the best one ever made—was still to come. It must have been exciting thinking about that candle. And I wonder what the people must have felt when the prophet Jonah told them to turn back to God and be sorry for what they'd done. I wonder if they were excited thinking about the Messiah and when he would arrive. I wonder.

Suggested prayer

Lord God, thank you for candles and the light they make. Thank you, too, for the story of the candle-maker. As we look at this yellow candle, we remember how important it is to be sorry when we do wrong things. We remember how we must give up wrong things and turn back to God. Help us to hear the message of the prophets about someone special, who was still to come; someone who would shine as the light for the whole world. Amen

The candle-maker: Week Three

Bible link

This week's Bible passage link is Hosea 14:4, which recounts the mercy of God when his people turned to him.

Key theme

This week's key theme is 'forgiveness', exploring what it feels like to be forgiven, and how easy or difficult it is to forgive others. How should we respond to others who repent? Is it right to forgive the candle-maker or should she be punished?

Episode Three

(Light the cracked and yellow candles.) Do you remember the story we're hearing? What were these candles used for? And was one of them the best candle ever made?

I hope you remember that this story reminds us about the prophets in the Bible. The message the mirror brought, saying that the candle-maker was right to feel sorry, is like the message from the prophet Jonah, who said, 'Pray to the Lord God with all your heart and stop being sinful and cruel.' In the Bible, though, the greatest of the prophets was called John the Baptist and he said, 'Someone more powerful is going to come.' I wonder who he meant.

The little mouse and the candle-maker rushed to see what had arrived through the letterbox. It was only the newspaper, but suddenly the candle-maker's heart seemed to miss a beat.

She'd just noticed the main headline. It said, 'Robbery at the palace! Police hunt for the criminals!' She was horrified. Maybe the police were looking for her now! She read some more of the story. It said that the police couldn't understand how the robbers had got into such a dark building unless they'd had a special kind of light.

The candle-maker put the newspaper down and thought about what to do. She ought to tell the police about the candle she'd made, but then she might be locked up in prison. Just then, she noticed the two candles she'd made. Next to the cracked one was the yellow candle, and she remembered how sorry she was for what she'd done. Then she knew she must go straight to the police station and tell them everything.

Once she was there, she told the policeman how she'd made the cracked candle for the robbers, and how she was very sorry for what she'd done. The policeman frowned. 'This is serious,' he said. 'I'm going to have to lock you up in my cell.' So the candle-maker sat in the little room, all alone, feeling very worried. What would happen now? Would she ever be able to make another candle again?

Finally, the policeman came back, but this time he had a big smile on his face. 'You did the right thing, coming to tell us what you'd done,' he said. 'You're forgiven! Everything that was stolen has been found. We're not going to put you in prison.' The candle-maker was so delighted that she danced out of the little room and started to leave the police station. By now, though, it was dark and she couldn't see which way to go home. 'Why not take this special silver candle?' said the policeman. 'Then you'll be able to see your way home safely.' The candle-maker laughed with delight. It was a candle that she herself had made for the police station. *(Show the silver candle and ask one of the children to help light it.)* She held it up high and it gave plenty of light for her as she went safely home.

When she got home, she had an idea. 'Maybe this is the most special and precious candle ever made,' she said to herself. 'I must ask the mirror!' So she carried the candle over to the mysterious mirror. After a few moments, the mirror began to speak. 'This is indeed a lovely candle, because you used it when you'd been completely forgiven. But this candle is not the most special and precious candle ever made. Another one, even better, is still to come.' Then the mirror stopped talking. The candle-maker was thinking about what the mirror had said when she heard something land on the doormat. 'I wonder what it is this time,' she said to herself.

I haven't got time to tell you any more of my story today, but maybe next time we'll find out what had just come through the letterbox. It's a very special story that I'm telling, because it reminds us about God and his own people, the Israelites. They were waiting and waiting for a very special person, called the Messiah, just like the candle-maker who was waiting to see if the candle she held in front of the mirror was the most special and precious one ever made. God's prophets kept telling the Israelites about the Messiah. One of them was the prophet Hosea, and he said, 'God's anger is gone and he will love you without limit', because that's what God does. The greatest of the prophets was called John the Baptist, but even he said, 'Someone more powerful is going to come', just as the mirror told the candle-maker that an even better candle was still to come.

I wonder what it would have been like to have been the candle-maker. It would have been fun making candles, and very special to use the silver candle. I wonder how she felt when the mirror said it wasn't the best one, the one she'd been hoping for, and that another one—the best one ever made—was still to come. It must have been exciting thinking about that candle. And I wonder what God's special people, the Israelites, must have felt when the prophet Hosea told them that God's anger was gone and that he loved them without limit. I wonder if they were excited, thinking about the Messiah and when he would arrive. I wonder.

Suggested prayer

Lord God, thank you for candles and the light they make. Thank you, too, for the story of the candle-maker. As we look at this silver candle, we remember how much you love us and we remember that you are never angry with us. Help us to hear the message of the prophets about someone special who was still to come, someone who would shine as the light for the whole world. Amen

*

The candle-maker: Week Four

Bible link

This week's Bible passage link is Ezekiel 36:26, which recounts the way in which God gave his people a new heart when they were reconciled to him.

Key theme

This week's key theme is 'celebration'. This is a big idea to explore and can include anything from the nature of celebration, to ways in which we celebrate, times when we celebrate and an exploration of the celebrations of Christianity and other faiths, especially celebrations taking place at this time of year. It is a good idea to think about how the ways in which people celebrate link with the event being celebrated.

Episode Four

(Light the cracked, yellow and silver candles.) Do you remember the story we're hearing? What were these candles used for? And was one of them the best candle ever made?

The story reminds us about the prophets in the Bible. The message that the mirror brought, saying how wonderful it is to be completely forgiven, is like the message from the prophet Hosea, who said, 'God's anger is gone and he will love you without limit.' In the Bible, though, the greatest of the prophets was called John the Baptist, and he said, 'Someone more powerful is going to come.' I wonder who he meant.

Do you remember? Something had just come through the letterbox, so the little mouse ran to see what it was. He came back very excited, so the candle-maker went to the door and saw that a letter had arrived. There was a big stamp in the corner of the envelope and her name and address were beautifully handwritten. She opened the envelope carefully and saw that the letter was from an old friend of hers, from the town where she used to live a long time ago.

There was so much news in the letter, about all the people in her home town and things that were happening there. The harvest had been very rich and even the poorest people had plenty to eat. Everyone was very happy and there were never any arguments. 'Oh, I wish I could be back there,' said the candle-maker to herself.

She kept on reading the letter. Her friend was having a great time. He'd turned one of the rooms in his house into a giant playroom, full of toys and games—and even had a candle-making kit. He was enjoying himself every day without worrying about anything at all. 'Oh, I wish I could be back there with my friend!' said the candle-maker to herself as she read.

Then she turned over the page and read something that made her very excited. Her friend had written, 'I promise to come and visit you next week—it will be so good to see you!' The candle-maker was so happy. 'If my friend comes to visit me, that will be just as good as me going back to be with him,' she said to herself with a laugh.

Then she had a really good idea. She would make another candle to celebrate the visit of her friend! She went into her candle-making room and melted some wax carefully in a pan. She decided to add some glitter. Then she poured the glittery wax carefully into the mould. When it had got cold again, she slowly took it out of the mould. *(Show the glittery candle and ask one of the children to help light it.)* It was a beautiful glittery candle and it made the candle-maker remember her friend's promise to visit.

Suddenly she had an idea. 'Maybe this is the most special and precious candle ever made,' she said to herself. 'I must ask the mirror!' So she carried the candle over to the mysterious mirror and waited for the mirror to say something. After a few moments, the mirror began to speak. 'This is indeed a beautiful glittery candle, one of the best I've seen, because it reminds you of your friend's promise. But this candle is not the most special and precious candle ever made. Another one, even better, is still to come.' Then the mirror stopped talking. The candle-maker was thinking about what the mirror had said when she heard the mouse squeaking at her and being very noisy. 'What is it?' asked the candle-maker. 'What's the matter?'

I haven't got time to tell you any more of my story today, but next time we'll find out why the mouse was so worried. It's a very special story that I'm telling, because it reminds us about God and his own people, the Israelites. They were waiting and waiting for a very special person, called the Messiah. God sent people called 'prophets' to tell the Israelites how much he loved them and to tell them about the Messiah. One of them was the prophet Ezekiel, and he said, 'God will give you a new heart', which means a heart that wants to be close to God. That's what God promises for us, too. It's a bit like the promise that the candle-maker's friend made to her. The greatest of the prophets was called John the Baptist, but even he said, 'Someone more powerful is going to come', just as the mirror told the candle-maker that an even better candle was still to come.

I wonder what it would have been like to have been the candle-maker. It would have been fun making candles, and very special to make the glittery candle. I wonder how she felt when the mirror said it wasn't the best one, the one she'd been hoping for. Maybe she was a little bit disappointed—but another one, the best one ever made, was still to come. It must have been exciting thinking about that candle. And I wonder what God's special people, the Israelites, must have felt when the prophet Ezekiel told them that God had promised to give them a new heart. I wonder if they were excited thinking about the Messiah and when he would arrive. I wonder.

Suggested prayer

Lord God, thank you for candles and the light they make. Thank you, too, for the story of the candle-maker. As we look at this glittery candle, we remember your promise to us that you will give us a new heart—a heart that wants to be close to you. Help us to hear the message of the prophets about someone special who was still to come, someone who would shine as the light for the whole world. Amen

The candle-maker: Week Five

Bible link

This week's Bible passage link is Isaiah 40:3, which recounts the way in which God's people needed to clear a pathway for him.

Key theme

This week's key theme is 'preparation'. As preparation was a theme at the very beginning of term, this time we focus on preparations for Christmas. Pupils can consider how the anticipation and excitement they feel as Christmas draws near is like what the candle-maker was feeling, waiting for her friend to arrive.

Episode Five

(*Light the cracked, yellow, silver and glittery candles.*) Do you remember the story we're hearing? What were these candles used for? And was one of them the best candle ever made?

The story reminds us about the prophets in the Bible, and how the message the mirror brought, speaking about the special promise made by the candle-maker's friend, is like the message from the prophet Ezekiel, who said, 'God will give you a new heart.' In the Bible, though, the greatest of the prophets was called John the Baptist, and he said, 'Someone more powerful is going to come.' I wonder who he meant.

Do you remember that the little mouse was really worried about something? The candle-maker couldn't understand it. 'Maybe the mouse is hungry,' she thought to herself. So she went and fetched a delicious bit of cheese, but he pushed it away with his nose and kept on squeaking. He wasn't hungry at all. 'Maybe the wax we need to make candles with is about to run out,' thought the candle-maker. So she went to have a look, but there was plenty of wax.

Just then, the mouse ran around, all over the letter from the candle-maker's friend, squeaking even more loudly. 'That letter isn't anything to get worried about,' said the candle-maker. 'It's a wonderful promise! It will be so good to welcome my friend here.' But suddenly she realised what the little mouse was so worried about. She hadn't had any visitors at her house for years and years. It was very messy and dusty and dirty. It needed tidying up and cleaning, if everything was to be prepared for her friend's visit.

The candle-maker started by tidying away all her clothes and books, and all the boxes of wax. Then she got her duster out, and her brush and her mop. She cleaned all the floors and carpets and dusted all the furniture. She even cleaned all the windows, which had got very dirty. It took her all day but, when she'd finished, the whole house was transformed. Everything was brighter and cleaner.

'I know!' she said to herself. 'All I need to do to complete my preparations is to make another candle, one with a beautiful smell.' So she went into her candle-making room and melted some wax carefully in a pan. She added some special perfume. When it was all melted together, she poured the wax carefully into the mould. When it had got cold again, she slowly took it out of the mould. (Show the scented candle and ask one of the children to help light it.) The candle made a lovely smell, perfect for her clean house. The candle-maker smiled because all the preparations for her visitor were complete.

Then she had an idea. 'Maybe this is the most special and precious candle ever made,' she said to herself. 'I must ask the mirror!' So she carried the candle over to the mysterious mirror and waited for the mirror to say something. After a few moments, the mirror began to speak. 'This is indeed a beautifully scented candle, and it completes your preparations for your friend's visit, but this candle is not the most special and precious candle ever made. Another one, even better, is still to come.' Then the mirror stopped talking. The candle-maker was thinking about what the mirror had said when she heard the little mouse squeaking at her and being very noisy again. 'What is it?' asked the candle-maker. 'Why are you still so worried?'

I haven't got time to tell you any more of my story today, but next time we'll find out why the mouse was still so worried. It's a very special story that I'm telling, because it reminds us about God and his own people, the Israelites. They were waiting and waiting for a very special person, called the Messiah, just like the candle-maker who was waiting to see if the candle she held in front of the mirror was the most special and precious one ever made. God sent people called 'prophets' to tell the Israelites how much he loved them and to tell them about the Messiah. One of them was the prophet Isaiah, who said, 'Clear a pathway for God.' That's what we must do to make sure we're prepared when God arrives. It's a bit like the scented candle, which completed the candle-maker's preparations. The greatest of the prophets was called John the Baptist, but even he said, 'Someone more powerful is going to come', just as the mirror told the candle-maker that an even better candle was still to come.

I wonder what it would have been like to have been the candle-maker. It would have been fun making candles, and very special to make the scented candle. I wonder how she felt when the mirror said it wasn't the best one, the one she'd been hoping for, and that another one—the best one ever made—was still to come. It must have been exciting thinking about that candle. And I wonder what God's special people, the Israelites, must have felt when the prophet Isaiah told them to clear a pathway for God. I wonder if they were excited thinking about the Messiah and when he would arrive. I wonder.

Suggested prayer

Lord God, thank you for candles and the light they make. Thank you, too, for the story of the candle-maker. As we smell this scented candle, we remember that we must be prepared for you. Help us to clear a pathway for you so that everything is ready. And help us to hear the message of the prophets about someone special who was still to come, someone who would shine as the light for the whole world. Amen

*

The candle-maker: Week Six

Bible link

This week's Bible passage link is Mark 1:4–8, especially verse 7, which recounts the message of John the Baptist that God's chosen Messiah is soon to arrive.

Key theme

This week's key theme is 'welcoming'. The candle-maker was keen to have everything ready so that her friend would feel welcome. How are people welcomed and made to feel at home? How do we welcome newcomers and visitors to our school?

Episode Six

(*Light the cracked, yellow, silver, glittery and scented candles.*) Do you remember the story we're hearing? What were these candles used for? And was one of them the best candle ever made?

The story reminds us about the prophets in the Bible and the message the mirror brought, saying that the way the candle-maker completed her preparations for her friend's visit is like the message from the prophet Isaiah, who said, 'Clear a pathway for God.' In the Bible, though, the greatest of the prophets was called John the Baptist, and he said, 'Someone more powerful is going to come.' I wonder who he meant.

The little mouse was still really worried about something, but the candle-maker couldn't understand why. 'What else could I possibly need to get ready?' she said, but the mouse ran right through the house into the candle-maker's bedroom and scurried around on her bed. 'Be careful!' shouted the candle-maker. 'Don't spoil my bed! That's where I sleep.' Suddenly she realised what the little mouse was so worried about. She didn't have a spare bed for her special visitor! Where could he possibly sleep?

The candle-maker tried to think what she could do to make a bed. To start with, she put some cushions and pillows on the floor. They looked quite good but when she actually tried them out by lying on them, they were very uncomfortable. 'That won't do,' she said. 'I'll have to think of something else.'

Then she remembered her rocking chair, where she liked to sit when she was resting. 'I always fall asleep in that chair,' she said to herself. 'Maybe that would do as a bed for my visitor, and I could put a blanket over it as well.' So she tried it out but it didn't really make a proper bed, and it kept on moving backwards and forwards. 'No, that won't do,' she said. 'I'll have to think of something else.'

The mouse was still on her bed but he was lying down and dozing now. That gave the candle-maker an idea. 'Maybe I could put my own mattress on the floor and my special visitor could sleep on it.' So that's what she did, and it was perfect. 'I know!' she said to herself. 'All I need to do to make the bed completely ready for my visitor is to make a bedside candle.' So she went into her candle-making room and melted some wax carefully in a pan, and when it was ready she poured it carefully into the mould. When it had got cold again, she slowly took it out of the mould. *(Show the purple candle and ask one of the children to help light it.)* It was a beautiful purple candle, just right to put by her visitor's bed. It made the candle-maker smile, because now everything was ready.

She scratched her head and said to herself, 'Maybe this is the most special and precious candle ever made. I must ask the mirror. Surely this time it must be!' So she carried the candle over to the mysterious mirror and waited for it to say something. After a few moments, the mirror began to speak. 'This is a very special purple candle, perfect for a visitor to have by his bed. It shows how much care you've taken in getting everything ready, but still this candle is not the most special and precious candle ever made. Another one, even better, is still to come.' Then the mirror stopped talking. The candle-maker couldn't understand. Surely this candle was the best one! Maybe the mirror had made a mistake? Just then, she stopped to listen carefully. She could hear footsteps outside and then there was a knock on the door.

My story's almost finished now, and next time I'm sure we'll find out who was knocking at the door. As you know, it's a very special story that I'm telling, because it reminds us about God and his own people, the Israelites. They were waiting and waiting for a very special person, called the Messiah, just like the candle-maker who was waiting to see if the candle she held in front of the mirror was the most special and precious one ever made. God sent people called 'prophets' to tell the Israelites how much he loved them and to tell them about the Messiah. The greatest of the prophets was called John the Baptist, but even he said, 'Someone more powerful is going to come', just as the mirror told the candle-maker that an even better candle was still to come.

I wonder what it would have been like to have been the candle-maker. It would have been fun making candles, and especially the purple bedside candle. But I wonder how she felt when the mirror said it wasn't the best one, the one she'd been hoping for, and that another one—the best one ever made—was still to come. It must have been exciting thinking about that candle. And I wonder what God's special people, the Israelites, must have felt when the prophet John the Baptist said that someone even more powerful was coming after him. I wonder if they were excited thinking about the Messiah and when he would arrive. I wonder.

Suggested prayer

Lord God, thank you for candles and the light they make. Thank you, too, for the story of the candle-maker. As we look at this purple candle, the colour fit for a king, help us to welcome someone special into the world, someone who will shine as the light for the whole world. Amen

The candle-maker:
Concluding celebration

The story of the candle-maker ends with the Christmas celebration. You could plan a nativity play or a more traditional carol service. The concluding episode reminds us that people had been waiting patiently for Christmas for many generations.

Concluding episode

(*Light the cracked, yellow, silver, glittery, scented and purple candles.*) Can you remember what these candles mean in our story? And was one of them the best candle ever made?

The story reminds us about the prophets in the Bible. The greatest of the prophets was a man called John the Baptist, and he said, 'Someone more powerful is going to come.' I wonder who he meant. It must have been someone very special.

Do you remember that the candle-maker was still waiting to show the most special and precious candle of all to the mysterious mirror? Every time she asked the mirror, it said that an even more special candle was still to come.

Then there was a knock at the door. 'It must be my friend, surely!' said the candle-maker to herself. She remembered what fun they used to have all those years ago, when she still lived in her home town, where everything was perfect. He was such a good friend, always kind and gentle and very strong. She could remember just what he looked like, even though she hadn't seen him for ages.

The candle-maker smiled as she thought how perfect it

would be to have her friend to stay. She opened the door, full of excitement, but it wasn't her friend at all. It was a little boy carrying a great big bag. The candle-maker was very disappointed. 'Oh dear!' she said. 'I thought you were an old friend of mine. I was expecting him today.'

Just then, the candle-maker saw the mouse rush out of the door and jump up, right into the little boy's hand. She looked at the boy's face again and she thought perhaps she'd seen it before. 'Did you get my letter?' the boy asked. 'Yes, I got the letter,' said the candle-maker. 'I mean, no! It wasn't from you. It was from my friend.' The candle-maker was getting more and more confused. 'At least, I didn't think the letter was from you. I thought it was from an old friend of mine, much older than you.'

The little boy smiled. 'That old friend of yours is my dad! We've got exactly the same name, so you must have got us muddled up. But he knew you'd be pleased to see me. He knew you'd love to have me to stay.' The candle-maker smiled as well. She was delighted. No wonder the boy looked familiar. 'Come along in!' she shouted. 'Everything is ready.' Together with the mouse, she showed her guest around.

The little boy loved seeing all the candles, and the candle-maker explained about each one. 'This cracked one was used for something very wrong,' she said, 'and I made this yellow one when I was feeling very sorry about what I'd done. Then I used this silver candle just when I knew I'd been completely forgiven.' The boy nodded with a smile each time the candle-maker told more of the story.

'Then, later, I got the letter with your promise to visit, and I made this glittery candle to celebrate, but I had to tidy everything up to prepare for when you arrived, so I made this scented candle to complete my preparations. And last of all, I made you a bed with this purple candle next to it.'

Then the candle-maker frowned and a sad note entered her voice. 'I kept thinking I'd made the perfect candle,' she said, 'so I took each one to the mysterious mirror to see what it would say. Every time, it told me that another candle, even more special, was still to come.' A little tear appeared at the corner of the candle-maker's eye as she realised that she hadn't managed to make the most special candle of all.

The little boy wiped the tear away from her eye. 'I can see how important that candle would be,' he said. 'Wouldn't it be amazing if we could really show it to the mirror?' Then he looked carefully in his bag and pulled out a beautiful tall white candle. *(Show the tall white candle and ask one of the children to help light it.)* The candle-maker gasped with delight and took it straight over to the mirror. There was a long pause, but finally the mirror began to speak. 'This is the most special and precious candle ever made! It's the one I've been waiting to see!'

The candle-maker laughed with joy. She realised that the thing she'd been waiting for had happened, and she had a very special friend with her, so she never needed to be lonely again. The wonderful tall white candle made everything complete.

This tall white candle reminds us of Jesus. He was the Messiah, the one whom all the prophets were looking forward to, and he is the true light for the world. That's why we celebrate Christmas, because we remember the time when Jesus was born, the time that all the prophets were waiting for, just like the candle-maker who waited and waited for the perfect candle. When Jesus arrives, we know that God really is with us.

*

The candle-maker:
Ideas for classroom follow-up

Alongside the main weekly assembly, you can develop the themes in the story in your classroom. One or more of the following ideas could be used.

- Explore stories about the prophets included in the story, especially John the Baptist.
- Think about how we decide what is right and wrong and how we can be influenced to do either. Consider why we often give into temptation even when we know it's wrong, and link this with discussions about our conscience.
- Consider the range of strong feelings illustrated in the story, drawing parallels with pupils' own experiences and the experiences of people they know, as well as characters in stories. These feelings might include loneliness, repentance (a change of heart), putting things right, forgiveness, wishing, anticipation and excitement.
- The candle-maker's friend made her a promise. Talk about keeping and breaking promises, making links with one of the term's values—trust.
- Explore the values of patience and trust.
- Find out about Advent customs. Make links between the candles in the story and the fact that many Christians and churches use candles as part of their Advent preparations and celebrations.
- Give thought towards the end of term to how the school, families and pupils themselves are getting ready for Christmas.

Within the curriculum you could make links with science, art, geography, literacy, PHSE, Citizenship and RE. You can find ideas on the website, www.barnabasinschools.org.uk/schools6993.

*

The discipleship parables

Key Bible verse

Jesus said, 'I have explained the secrets about
the kingdom of heaven to you.'
MATTHEW 13:11

Values

Love and honesty

This section is designed to run from January until the February
break. The theme is the discipleship parables and, in the big story
of God's love for the world, we are remembering the ways that Jesus
taught us how to live our lives. When we imagine ourselves within
this part of the story, we discover different things we can do that
help us grow closer to God.

The story of Cassandra's crown is told in six parts as an
illustration of the discipleship parables of Jesus, which are found
in the Gospels.

- Week One: Matthew 13:10–17
- Week Two: The parable of the two sons (Luke 15:11–32)
- Week Three: The parable of the good Samaritan (Luke 10:30–37)
- Week Four: The parable of the workers in the vineyard (Matthew 20:1–16)
- Week Five: The parable of the three servants (Matthew 25:14–30)
- Week Six: The parable of the valuable pearl (Matthew 13:45–46)

The storyteller's prop used for the story consists of:

- A crown
- Five imitation jewels mounted on letter shapes with magnetic backing
- A plain cardboard box that the crown fits snugly within

The crown should be distinctive enough to look special. It must also be made at least partly of metal so that the magnetic 'jewels' can be held in place on the crown but easily removed. One suggestion is to make the crown using an empty sweet tin (the kind that is round and holds about 1 kg of sweets). These are widely available at Christmas time. If the tin, without its lid, is held upside down, it makes an excellent basis for the crown and will hold the magnets. The tin can be embellished with crenellations made from sticks or cardboard. The whole crown can then be covered with a thin layer of newspaper soaked in wallpaper paste, allowed to dry and then spray-painted silver or gold. A thin strip of imitation ermine-style fur could be used to trim the crown.

At the start of the story, the crown is in a cardboard box. The five jewels should be as light as possible. For the first four, one idea is to find some party bag novelty rings that have plastic gems mounted on them. These can be removed easily from the rings and stuck on to the letter shapes. The fifth is a pearl, and this could be made from a small spherical object, perhaps the top of a small shampoo bottle, painted a suitable shiny colour.

The five jewels are as follows:

- Red gem (ruby): letter 'e' shape
- Green gem (emerald): letter 'u' shape
- Blue gem (sapphire): letter 's' shape
- Purple gem (amethyst): letter 'J' shape
- Pearl: letter 's' shape

The letter shapes need to be mounted on to magnetic backing. One way to do this is to use a magnetic learner driver L-plate and cut pieces from it as required. These can be stuck to the reverse of the letter shapes. Once completed, the letters need to attach to the crown and hold in place. A photograph of an example of the crown prop can be found on the website, www.barnabasinschools.org.uk/schools6993.

Suggested music

Suggestions for pre-recorded music that could be used at the start and end of assemblies include:

- *The Lord of the Rings (Fellowship of the Ring)* soundtrack (Howard Shore, Reprise Records WMG948110-2)
- 'The bridge of Khazad Dum' (track 13) (used at the start)
- 'Concerning hobbits' (track 2) (used at the end)

Suggestions for songs that could be sung at assemblies include:

- Abba, Father, let me be (Week Six) (JP 2)
- Father, I place into your hands (JP 42)
- I will make you fishers of men (JP 123)
- If I were a butterfly (Week Four) (JP 94)
- Make me a channel of your peace (JP 161)
- One more step along the world I go (JP 188)
- Seek ye first the kingdom of God (JP 215)
- Thank you, Lord, for this fine day (JP 232)
- When I needed a neighbour (Week Three) (JP 275)

Cassandra's crown: Week One

Bible link

This week's Bible passage link is Matthew 13:10–17, which explains why Jesus taught using parables, so that the secrets of the kingdom of heaven might become known.

Key theme

This week's key theme is 'learning from stories'. Jesus used stories to help people understand his challenging messages. Sometimes stories can simplify or clarify ideas. They can also bring to life difficult teachings, helping people to understand the impact of behaviours and actions. They are often easier to listen to than information or lectures.

Episode One

I wonder if you like exploring and going on adventures to discover new things. Today I want to start telling you a new story about a girl called Cassandra. She loved adventures and exploring, and she was about the same age as you. In fact, it's a very special story, because in a funny kind of way it tells us about God.

One day, a quiet day when nothing much seemed to be happening, Cassandra was upstairs at home. She decided to explore the spare room, where everyone just dumped things when they couldn't think of anywhere better to put them. It was a very dusty room and there were boxes piled up all over the place. Some of them weren't very interesting. One was an old shoebox. Another was the box for a television, which had been new last Christmas. But over in the furthest corner there was an interesting box that Cassandra hadn't seen before (*show the box*).

Somehow, she managed to clamber over all the rubbish in the room and carefully picked up the box. It felt quite heavy. She felt sure that something very special was inside. Holding her breath, she opened the top of the box. Then she gasped with amazement because inside the box was an ancient crown (*take the crown out of the box*).

The crown was made of metal, with some fur around the bottom, but it was quite plain. It didn't have any gems or jewels in it. As she held it up, it caught the light and the metal glinted at Cassandra. Now she could see it was gold! She wondered who the crown was for—perhaps a king of some kind? Then she had an idea. She would try it on herself and see if it fitted her. It was quite an effort to lift the crown up, ready to put on to her own head, but eventually she managed it. She paused for a moment. Would anything special happen, she wondered? Or maybe it would be dangerous to wear such a strange thing. Then she laughed to herself. 'No, of course nothing will happen. It's probably just part of an old fancy-dress costume that Grandma must have made years ago.' She wasn't completely sure but, even so, she put it on (*mime putting the crown on*).

Suddenly there was a peculiar rushing noise in her ears and the room seemed to be swirling around her in a blur. Everything was moving and changing but she wasn't scared. She felt quite safe. After a few moments, all the movement and the noise seemed to stop again, but the dusty old room at the end of the upstairs hall had gone. Instead, she was in a bigger room with a high ceiling and no windows. The walls were all made of rough stone and it felt as though the room could be underground. A big lantern was hanging on a rope, lighting up the room. Then Cassandra noticed a funny little person, like an elf, walking in through an open doorway. He stopped with a startled look on his face. 'Oh! You must be trying to find out the secret of the crown,' he said in a squeaky voice.

Cassandra nodded nervously and the little elf-like man continued, 'Well, you'll have to go down that passageway over there.' He pointed towards an exit from the room. 'But I warn you, it's very difficult to discover the secret of the crown. Many try and fail.' He looked at Cassandra thoughtfully for a moment. 'Of course, you could decide to take the crown off straight away and go back. That would be much safer, but it would be a shame as well, because you'd never discover the secret of the crown if you did. If you keep the crown on, you might discover loads of exciting things. Good luck!' And he disappeared through another of the exits.

Cassandra stood still, looking up at the ceiling of the room, wondering what was going on. 'I must be in a dream,' she said to herself, 'but it feels completely real. Maybe I really can discover the secret of the crown. Or maybe I should just take the crown off…'

Next week we'll find out what Cassandra decided to do. It's a very special story I've started telling, because it reminds us about God and his heavenly kingdom. You see, the kingdom of heaven is a mysterious thing. It's a bit like a secret. In fact, Jesus once said to his disciples, 'I have explained the secrets about the kingdom of heaven to you', but not everyone understands, a bit like Cassandra in the story. She will have to go through lots of adventures in order to discover the secret of the crown, just as the people who follow Jesus have to understand lots of things in order to discover the secrets of the kingdom of heaven.

I wonder what it would have been like to put on the old crown and go into an adventure. I wonder what the secret of the crown is. And I wonder what it was like for the disciples to hear about the secrets of the kingdom of heaven from Jesus. I wonder what it would have been like to be there as well, listening to Jesus explaining those secrets. I wonder.

Suggested prayer

Lord God, thank you for adventures when we discover new things, sometimes secret things that many people don't know. Thank you for the story about Cassandra and the secret of the crown, and thank you that Jesus taught people about the secrets of the kingdom of heaven. Help us to understand more and more about those secrets, so that we can belong in that kingdom as well. Amen

The Lord's Prayer is also especially suitable. Either the traditional or contemporary wording can be used.

Our Father, who art in heaven,
hallowed be thy name.
Thy kingdom come,
thy will be done,
on earth as it is in heaven.
Give us this day our daily bread.
And forgive us our trespasses,
as we forgive those
who trespass against us.
And lead us not into temptation,
but deliver us from evil.

For thine is the kingdom,
the power, and the glory,
for ever and ever. Amen

Our Father in heaven,
hallowed be your name.
Your kingdom come,
your will be done,
on earth as in heaven.
Give us today our daily bread.
Forgive us our sins
as we forgive those
who sin against us.
Save us from the time of trial,
and deliver us from evil.
For the kingdom, the power
and the glory are yours,
now and for ever. Amen

Cassandra's crown: Week Two

Bible link

This week's Bible passage link is Luke 15:11–32, the parable of the two sons, sometimes called the parable of the loving father.

Key theme

This week's key theme is 'saying sorry'. Sometimes it's very hard to say sorry and admit mistakes, but it is important in the process of putting things right. The parable of the two sons is also about the forgiveness and love of the father and links with one of the values associated with this theme.

Episode Two

(*Show the crown.*) Can you remember whose crown this is? What happened when Cassandra put it on? Do you think she will ever find out the secret of the crown?

The story tells us something about God and Jesus. Can you remember what the secrets were that Jesus talked about? I wonder if those secrets were like the secret of the crown.

Cassandra loved adventures and, although the little elf had said it would be very difficult to discover the secret of the crown, she decided to keep on going down the passageway. After a long walk, she arrived at a door. Suddenly it flew open and a kind old man with a big white beard appeared. 'You must be Cassandra,' he said gently. 'I've been expecting you.'

Cassandra stumbled into the room and gasped. There on a

big wooden table was a great pile of all her favourite sweets—
toffee chews, marshmallow delights, fudge, and mint chocolates.
'They're all yours,' said the old man with the white beard, 'but
don't waste them. They're very important if you're going to find
out the secret of the crown.'

Cassandra's eyes lit up as she scooped the pile of sweets into
her bag. Then she waved goodbye to the old man and continued
down the passageway. As she walked, she decided to eat just
one of the sweets, a lovely mint chocolate. It was delicious, and
before she knew it she'd eaten another three. In fact, they were
so nice that she searched in the bag until she'd found every last
mint chocolate and eaten them all. Cassandra kept on walking
but she still felt hungry. 'Just one toffee chew wouldn't hurt,'
she said to herself and popped it into her mouth. It was even
more delicious than the mint chocolates. Before long, she'd
eaten all the toffee chews, and the marshmallow delights, and
even the fudge. Suddenly Cassandra began to feel very sad. 'I'll
never find out the secret of the crown, now I've wasted all the
sweets,' she sobbed.

Cassandra thought about what she could do. Maybe she
could pretend that there was a hole in the bag and that the
sweets had all dropped out? Or perhaps she could tell everyone
that a thief had stolen them? Eventually, she decided what to do.
She got up and started walking back towards the room where
the old man had given her all the sweets. Soon she saw the
doorway up ahead but, before she even got close, the old man
with the big white beard rushed out. 'Cassandra!' he smiled
at her. 'I'm so pleased to see you again!' But Cassandra shook
her head sadly. 'I've done something really bad,' she said. 'I've
wasted all those sweets you gave me, which were supposed to

help me discover the secret of the crown. I ate every one.' She looked down at the floor. 'I'm sorry,' she said. 'I've made a bad mistake, and I've come back to say sorry.'

The old man looked serious. 'Those sweets were very special,' he said, 'but I'm pleased you came back. I'm pleased you didn't try to blame someone else, and I'm very pleased you said sorry.' Cassandra felt a warm glow inside her and she shut her eyes. When she opened them again, the old man with the white beard had gone and the little elf had appeared instead. He was pointing at the crown. 'You've started learning about the secret of the crown,' he said. 'Look!' *(Show crown with red gem added.)* On the crown, a beautiful sparkling red ruby had appeared. 'You know about going back and saying sorry when things go wrong,' said the elf. 'That's what the red gem means! But you haven't discovered everything about the secret of the crown yet—not by a long way.'

Next time, we'll hear some more about Cassandra and the crown. It's a very special story because it reminds us of what Jesus said about the kingdom of heaven. Jesus told a parable about a man who took all his inheritance, all the things that he'd been given, and wasted them, just like Cassandra wasted all those sweets—but the man went back and said sorry to his father. Jesus tells us that's what God wants us to be like, if we want to understand the secrets about the kingdom of heaven. When things go wrong, we must always turn back to God our heavenly Father and say sorry. The red ruby on Cassandra's crown reminds us of that.

In fact, Jesus once said to his disciples, 'I have explained the secrets about the kingdom of heaven to you', but not everyone understands, a bit like Cassandra and the secret of the crown.

She'll have to keep going through her adventure to discover the secret of the crown, just as the people who follow Jesus have to understand lots of things to discover the secrets of the kingdom of heaven.

I wonder what it was like for Cassandra to go back and say sorry when she made that mistake. I wonder what the secret of the crown is. And I wonder what it was like for the disciples to hear about the secrets of the kingdom of heaven from Jesus. I wonder what it would have been like to be there as well, listening to Jesus explaining those secrets. I wonder.

Suggested prayer

Lord God, thank you for adventures when we discover new things, sometimes secret things that many people don't know. Thank you for the story about Cassandra and the secret of the crown, with its new red gem, and the way she discovered about going back to say sorry. Thank you that Jesus taught people about the secrets of the kingdom of heaven. Help us to understand more and more about those secrets, so that we can belong in that kingdom as well. Amen

The Lord's Prayer is also especially suitable (see pages 84–85).

Cassandra's crown: Week Three

Bible link

This week's Bible passage link is Luke 10:30–37, the parable of the good Samaritan.

Key theme

This week's key theme is 'helping others'. The challenge of the parable of the good Samaritan is not about just helping others but helping those we feel least inclined to help. Who are the outcasts in our society today—those we might feel uncomfortable with or prejudiced against? Explore examples of good Samaritans in our society who help these people; then reflect on who we would find it difficult to help and how we could overcome these feelings. Consideration may need to be given to contexts when it would be unwise for children to go directly to the aid of people in need. Why, and what else could they do instead?

Episode Three

(*Show the crown.*) Can you remember whose crown this is? And what does this red ruby mean?

The story tells us something about God and Jesus. Can you remember what the secrets were that Jesus talked about? I wonder if those secrets were like the secret of the crown.

The little elf pointed down one of the passageways. 'Be careful!' he said. 'Don't be distracted from your journey to find out the secret of the crown.' So Cassandra stumbled down the passageway, which gradually curved round to the left. As she tiptoed onwards, she noticed something in the way. It looked like a sack of potatoes.

Suddenly, the strange sack moved and made a groaning sound, like a person who'd been injured. The person rolled over and, as Cassandra saw the face, she froze with horror. It was a girl called Cruella, who was horrible to everyone at school but especially to Cassandra. Just last week, Cassandra had brought a special peacock's feather into school to show everyone, but Cruella had snapped it in two; and last term Cruella had put a worm on Cassandra's plate at lunch! Cruella was definitely Cassandra's worst enemy. 'I've got to carry on to find out the secret of the crown,' Cassandra said to herself. 'I mustn't get distracted.' So she stepped carefully past. She noticed that Cruella had a big cut on her head and bruises everywhere. 'Serves you right!' she thought to herself.

The passageway kept curving round to the left, on and on. Then Cassandra stopped again. There was something else blocking the way, like a bundle of clothes on the floor. Cassandra crept forward very cautiously. The bundle started to move and a voice said, 'Help me! Help me, please!' Cassandra froze to the spot. It was Cruella's voice! The passageway must have gone round in a big circle. Cruella was looking up at her with a pleading expression. 'Please help me,' she said. 'I'm hurting badly.' Cassandra thought quickly. 'I mustn't be distracted,' she said to herself. 'I must keep on going, so I can find out the secret of the crown. And anyway, she's my worst enemy.' So Cassandra hurried on her way.

The passageway kept on curving round and Cassandra kept on walking. But then she stopped. She couldn't believe her eyes. Cruella was there again, slumped on the floor. Cassandra paused. She knew she was supposed to carry on without stopping so that she could discover the secret of the crown, and she knew that Cruella was her worst enemy. She remembered the broken peacock feather and the worm on her plate, but she knew she couldn't leave Cruella like this. So she gently wiped Cruella's face and gave her a drink from her water bottle. Then she helped Cruella along the passageway.

Suddenly the walls weren't curving any more. There was a door ahead and the kind old man with the big white beard was there, giving Cruella some food. 'Please look after her,' said Cassandra. 'Keep my water bottle, so she can drink from it when she's thirsty.' The old man smiled. 'You did a very special thing back there, Cassandra,' he said. 'I'm very pleased with you.' Cassandra closed her eyes and felt a warm glow inside her. When she opened her eyes, the old man was gone, but the little elf had appeared. He was pointing excitedly. 'You're learning about the secret of the crown,' he said. 'Look!' *(Show the crown with green gem added.)* On the crown, a beautiful sparkling green emerald had appeared. 'You know about helping people when they're in trouble, even your worst enemy. That's what the green gem means! But you haven't discovered everything about the secret of the crown yet—not by a long way.'

Next time, we'll hear some more about Cassandra and the crown. It's a very special story because it reminds us what Jesus said about the kingdom of heaven. Jesus told a parable about a Jewish man who was attacked and robbed and left lying by the side of the road. Two people found him but they both walked past on the other side, just like when Cassandra crept past Cruella. The third person who found the injured man was a Samaritan, and he stopped to help even though the Jews and

Samaritans were enemies—just like when Cassandra stopped to help her worst enemy, Cruella. It's the parable of the good Samaritan, which tells us about caring for all our neighbours. That's what it's like in the kingdom of heaven, and the green emerald on Cassandra's crown reminds us of that.

In fact, Jesus once said to his disciples, 'I have explained the secrets about the kingdom of heaven to you', but not everyone understands, a bit like Cassandra and the secret of the crown. She'll have to keep going through her adventure to discover the secret of the crown, just as the people who follow Jesus have to understand lots of things to discover the secrets of the kingdom of heaven.

I wonder what it was like for Cassandra to help Cruella. Would you have done the same as her? I wonder what the secret of the crown is. And I wonder what it was like for the disciples to hear about the secrets of the kingdom of heaven from Jesus. I wonder what it would have been like, listening to Jesus explaining those secrets. I wonder.

Suggested prayer

Lord God, thank you for adventures when we discover new things, sometimes secret things that many people don't know. Thank you for the story about Cassandra and the secret of the crown, with its new green gem, and the way she discovered about helping her worst enemy. Thank you that Jesus taught people about the secrets of the kingdom of heaven. Help us to understand more and more about those secrets, so that we can belong in that kingdom as well. Amen

The Lord's Prayer is also especially suitable (see pages 84–85).

Cassandra's crown: Week Four

Bible link

This week's Bible passage link is Matthew 20:1–16, the parable of the workers in the vineyard.

Key theme

This week's key theme is 'equal but different'. Everyone is a child of God and, as such, loved by God despite the many differences between people and their different behaviours. Explore understandings and responses to other people and to God. Reflect on how this challenges people to treat others.

Episode Four

(Show the crown.) Can you remember what Cassandra is trying to discover? And what do the red ruby and the green emerald mean?

The story tells us something about God and Jesus. Can you remember what the secrets were that Jesus talked about? I wonder if those secrets were like the secret of the crown.

The little elf looked very seriously at Cassandra and said, 'You haven't discovered the whole secret of the crown yet. It's a very hard discovery to make and the next part of the adventure is even harder.' He pointed down another passageway. So Cassandra set off again. The passageway seemed to go deeper into the ground but suddenly she had to stop. There was a wall completely blocking the way. Just then, five animals arrived down the passageway. They were a dog, a cat, a horse, a kangaroo and a monkey. 'We know how to get past,' said the monkey. 'We must paint a really beautiful picture on the wall and then it will open.'

The kangaroo reached into its pouch for brushes and paint and the animals started work. Even Cassandra joined in and they made a good start, but quite soon Cassandra noticed that the monkey was starting to yawn. In another two minutes he'd dropped his paintbrush and was fast asleep on the floor. Cassandra couldn't wake him up, so she carried on painting with the other four animals.

Soon the kangaroo started yawning, and in no time he'd dropped his paintbrush and was fast asleep. The others kept painting, but then Cassandra saw that the horse was fast asleep as well. She began to worry about whether they would ever finish. A bit later, Cassandra looked round and saw the cat also fast asleep on the ground. Luckily, the dog was just making the finishing touches. It was a picture of a gong, which instantly made a crashing noise! All the animals woke up straight away and the wall started to open.

Cassandra saw the old man with the big white beard, with a smile on his gentle face. He had some golden badges in his hand. 'These are a reward for everyone who was a good helper,' he said. 'Cassandra, you must decide who will get one.' Cassandra took the badges. 'The dog should definitely get one,' she thought to herself, 'and probably the cat as well.' Then Cassandra looked at the horse. He was such a nice horse, so she decided to give him a golden badge, too. But the kangaroo had been asleep for most of the time. Surely he didn't really deserve to get a badge, did he? Eventually Cassandra gave a badge to the kangaroo, because he had helped a bit. Then Cassandra looked at the monkey. He was holding out his hand for a badge, even though he had hardly helped. What would the other animals think if she gave him one? Cassandra was about to say, 'No!' but at the last moment she gave the monkey a badge as well.

The old man smiled at Cassandra. 'You did just the right thing, giving everyone a badge even though they all helped for different amounts of time. I'm very pleased with you.' Cassandra closed her eyes and felt the warm glow inside her again. When she opened her eyes, the old man was gone, but the little elf was there, pointing. 'You're learning about the secret of the crown,' he squeaked. 'Look!' (*Show the crown with blue gem added.*) On the crown, a beautiful sparkling blue sapphire had appeared. 'You know that everyone is really equal, even if they seem to be different. That's what the blue gem means! But you haven't discovered everything about the secret of the crown yet.'

Next time, we'll hear some more about Cassandra and the crown. It's a very special story because it reminds us what Jesus said about the kingdom of heaven. Jesus told a parable about some workers in a vineyard. Some of them worked hard all day and others worked only for a short while, just like the animals doing the painting, but the owner of the vineyard paid all those workers the same amount, just like when Cassandra gave all the animals a golden badge. Jesus' story is called the parable of the workers in the vineyard, which tells us that we are all equal in God's eyes. That's what it's like in the kingdom of heaven, and the blue sapphire on Cassandra's crown reminds us of that.

In fact, Jesus once said to his disciples, 'I have explained the secrets about the kingdom of heaven to you', but not everyone understands, a bit like Cassandra and the secret of the crown.

She'll have to keep going through her adventure to discover the secret of the crown, just as the people who follow Jesus have to understand lots of things to discover the secrets of the kingdom of heaven.

I wonder what it was like for Cassandra when she had to decide who should have a golden badge. What would we have decided? I wonder what the secret of the crown really is. And I wonder what it was like for the disciples to hear about the secrets of the kingdom of heaven from Jesus. I wonder what it would have been like, listening to Jesus explaining those secrets. I wonder.

Suggested prayer

Lord God, thank you for adventures when we discover new things, sometimes secret things that many people don't know. Thank you for the story about Cassandra and the secret of the crown, with its new blue gem, and the way she discovered that everyone is equal. Thank you that Jesus taught people about the secrets of the kingdom of heaven. Help us to understand more and more about those secrets, so that we can belong in that kingdom as well. Amen

The Lord's Prayer is also especially suitable (see pages 84–85).

Cassandra's crown: Week Five

Bible link

This week's Bible passage link is Matthew 25:14–30, the parable of the three servants.

Key theme

This week's key theme is 'using our talents'. Everyone is good at something. Christians believe that God gives us all talents and he wants us to use them to live the very best lives we can. There are lots of opportunities to reflect on the talents of people within and outside school, and how the way they are used makes a difference to those individuals, the people around them and, in some cases, to the world.

Episode Five

(*Show the crown.*) Can you remember what Cassandra is trying to discover? And what do the red ruby, the green emerald and the blue sapphire mean?

The story tells us something about God and Jesus. Can you remember what the secrets were that Jesus talked about? I wonder if those secrets were like the secret of the crown.

The elf was playing a tune on an amazing musical instrument, a recorder made of pure gold. 'That must be worth a fortune!' said Cassandra. 'Yes,' replied the elf, as he handed it to her. 'It's worth at least one million pounds and you must keep it very safe.' So she locked the recorder in its case with three separate keys and hid it right at the bottom of her bag.

Cassandra set off again on her journey. The pathway ahead of her led into a maze and soon Cassandra was completely lost. Even worse, the hedges were full of growls and roars, and suddenly a furry hand reached out and tried to grab Cassandra's bag. She just managed to snatch it back in time. 'The golden recorder is in there,' she sobbed to herself. 'Whatever happens, I mustn't lose it, or I'll never find out the secret of the crown.' Cassandra started running through the maze. More and more furry hands were grabbing for her bag, so she threw it to the ground and sat down on top of it. 'That should be safe,' she gasped.

Then Cassandra got really worried about being lost. 'If only I had a compass, or a whistle to call for help,' she thought to herself, and started searching in her bag. She'd almost finished looking through the contents when she found the golden recorder. 'Thank goodness it's safe,' she said, and she put it quickly away again, down at the bottom of her bag. She knew she had to take care of it. She looked around and a tear started to roll down her cheek. She was stuck in this maze with no way of escaping. Now she'd never discover the secret of the crown. She felt in her bag one more time, slowly pulled out the recorder case and opened it up. The recorder gleamed brightly, but there was a growl from one of the hedges and she snapped the case shut quickly. Then she opened it again. She'd had an idea. Maybe she could play some music on the recorder to cheer herself up. As she played, the recorder made a beautiful sound.

Gradually, something amazing started to happen. The plants in the hedges seemed to be moving. At last she realised that there wasn't a maze any more, only a straight avenue of trees and shrubs leading her on. Cassandra kept on playing the golden recorder as she ran down the avenue. There at the end of the trees was the old man with the long white beard and the lovely smile. 'I'm so pleased you used that special gift I gave you and didn't just keep it hidden away,' he said. Cassandra closed her eyes and felt the warm glow inside her. When she opened her eyes again, the old man was gone, but the little elf was there, pointing at the crown, his eyes opened wide. 'You're learning about the secret of the crown,' he said. 'Look!' *(Show the crown with purple gem added.)* On the crown, a beautiful sparkling purple amethyst had appeared. 'You know that special gifts must be used and not hidden away. That's what the purple gem means. But you haven't quite discovered everything about the secret of the crown yet.'

Next time, we'll hear some more about Cassandra and the crown. It's a very special story because it reminds us what Jesus said about the kingdom of heaven. Jesus told a parable about three men who were each given precious gifts, just as Cassandra was given that golden recorder. One of the men was so worried about his precious gift that he buried it underground and kept it hidden, a bit like Cassandra kept the recorder hidden to start with. But the other men used their gifts well, just as Cassandra used the golden recorder to play a tune and continue her adventure. The story Jesus told is called the parable of the three servants, which tells us we must use the gifts that God has generously given us, because that's how we celebrate God's love for us. That's what it's like in the kingdom of heaven, and the purple amethyst on Cassandra's crown reminds us of that.

In fact, Jesus once said to his disciples, 'I have explained the secrets about the kingdom of heaven to you', but not everyone understands, a bit like Cassandra and the secret of the crown. She'll have to keep going through her adventure to discover the secret of the crown, just as the people who follow Jesus have to understand lots of things to discover the secrets of the kingdom of heaven.

I wonder what it was like for Cassandra when she risked getting out the golden recorder. Would we have done the same? I wonder what the secret of the crown really is. And I wonder what it was like for the disciples to hear about the secrets of the kingdom of heaven from Jesus. I wonder what it would have been like, listening to Jesus explaining those secrets. I wonder.

Suggested prayer

Lord God, thank you for adventures when we discover new things, sometimes secret things that many people don't know. Thank you for the story about Cassandra and the secret of the crown, with its new purple gem, and the way she discovered that gifts must be celebrated and used, not locked away. Thank you that Jesus taught people about the secrets of the kingdom of heaven. Help us to understand more and more about those secrets, so that we can belong in that kingdom as well. Amen

The Lord's Prayer is also especially suitable (see pages 84–85).

Cassandra's crown: Week Six

Bible link

This week's Bible passage link is Matthew 13:45–46, the parable of the valuable pearl.

Key theme

This week's key theme is 'commitment'. Christians believe that they should dedicate their lives to God and what he wants. Other people have other commitments and beliefs that inform their lives. Reflect on the things that are important to different people and the effects this has on their lives.

Episode Six

(Show the crown.) Can you remember what Cassandra is trying to discover? What do the red ruby, the green emerald, the blue sapphire and the purple amethyst mean?

The story tells us something about God and Jesus. Can you remember what the secrets were that Jesus talked about? I wonder if those secrets were like the secret of the crown.

The elf looked seriously at Cassandra. 'The old man gave me this to help you discover the secret of the crown,' he said, and he handed Cassandra a mysterious cloak, shimmering like a mirror. It was an invisibility cloak! So Cassandra set off and soon she came into a huge underground cave.

The pathway led to a bridge, guarded by three horrible goblins. Cassandra's heart sank, but then she remembered the invisibility cloak. She slipped it on and walked carefully towards the bridge. The goblins didn't notice her at all and she managed to creep past them, over the bridge. 'Maybe I'll discover the secret of the crown now,' she thought to herself.

But the pathway led to another, longer bridge, guarded by two big smelly trolls. Cassandra kept tiptoeing along, still wearing her invisibility cloak. The trolls were so fat that she couldn't squeeze past them, so she threw some pebbles and, while the trolls were distracted, she ran over the bridge as quickly as she could. 'Maybe now I'll discover the secret of the crown,' she thought to herself.

Still the pathway led on, winding through the enormous cave. Up ahead, Cassandra could see another, even longer bridge, guarded by a huge giant, about 20 feet tall. She still had her invisibility cloak on, but suddenly the giant roared, 'You can't get past me! Invisibility cloaks don't work against my eyes. If you want to pass, you must give me everything you have!'

Cassandra panicked and held out her lunchbox towards the giant. He grabbed it greedily and then roared, 'That's not enough! You must give me everything!' Cassandra was shaking all over but she pulled her favourite cuddly toy out of her bag. The giant grabbed it and roared, 'That's not enough! You must give me everything!' Cassandra was completely terrified now. She felt desperately in her bag and pulled out the golden recorder. Before she knew what was happening, the giant had grabbed it, roaring, 'That's not enough! You must give me everything!'

Just then, Cassandra remembered the invisibility cloak. She slipped it off her shoulders and held it out to the giant. The giant grinned at her, grabbed the cloak quickly and stuffed it in his pocket. Then he opened his mouth and said with a roar, 'That's not enough! You must give me everything!' Cassandra began to sob with tears. 'I haven't got anything else,' she cried. 'I so wanted to find out the secret of the crown and now I never will. There's nothing else I can do.' Cassandra found herself running towards the giant, knowing that she wouldn't survive, shouting, 'I'll have to give you my life!'

But then an amazing thing happened. As Cassandra crashed into the huge giant, there was a funny popping sound and he disappeared. Cassandra kept running over the bridge and, at the other side, the kind old man with the long white beard was waiting. He said to Cassandra, 'I'm very pleased that you got past the giant by being prepared to give up your whole life.' Cassandra closed her eyes and felt the warm glow inside her again. When she opened her eyes, the old man was still there, and with him was the little elf. 'You've almost learnt about the secret of the crown,' said the elf. 'Look!' *(Show the crown with pearl added.)* On the crown, a beautiful sparkling pearl had appeared. 'You know that to understand the secret of the crown you must be prepared to give everything, even your whole life. That's what the pearl means.'

The story has almost finished now, and next time we'll hear the very last bit. I hope that Cassandra will discover what the secret of the crown really is. It's a very special story because it reminds us what Jesus said about the kingdom of heaven. Jesus told a parable about someone who sold everything they had, so that they could buy a perfect pearl, just like when Cassandra gave up everything to the giant so that she could get over the bridge. The story Jesus told is called the parable of the valuable pearl, which tells us that we must be ready to give our whole lives to God without holding anything back. That's what it's like in the kingdom of heaven, and the perfect pearl on Cassandra's crown reminds us of that.

In fact, Jesus once said to his disciples, 'I have explained the secrets about the kingdom of heaven to you', but not everyone understands, a bit like Cassandra and the secret of the crown.

I wonder what it was like for Cassandra when she ran towards the giant. Would we have done the same? I wonder if we'll ever discover what the secret of the crown really is. And I wonder what it was like for the disciples to hear about the secrets of the kingdom of heaven from Jesus. I wonder what it would have been like, listening to Jesus explaining those secrets. I wonder.

Suggested prayer

Lord God, thank you for adventures when we discover new things, sometimes secret things that many people don't know. Thank you for the story about Cassandra and the secret of the crown, with its gems and pearl, and the way she discovered that she must be ready to give her whole life. Thank you that Jesus taught people about the secrets of the kingdom of heaven. Help us to understand more and more about those secrets, so that we can belong in that kingdom as well. Amen

The Lord's Prayer is also especially suitable (see pages 84–85).

Cassandra's crown:
Concluding celebration

The story of Cassandra's crown can end with a Christingle celebration. You could give the children their own Christingles or make one for everyone to look at. Details about making Christingles are available on The Children's Society website: www.childrenssociety.org.uk. Alternatively, you could make a connection to Pancake Day, which marks the start of Lent. The concluding episode of the story of Cassandra's crown reminds us that Christians believe Jesus is the person who shows us what the kingdom of heaven is like.

Concluding episode

(*Show the crown.*) I wonder if you remember the story of Cassandra, the girl who found this old and special crown in a box in the spare room at her home. Do you remember how she put the crown on and it transported her into an adventure through underground passageways and caves? Look! Here's the crown now, and it's covered in gems and jewels.

The first gem to appear on the crown was the red ruby, when Cassandra foolishly ate all the sweets she'd been given by the kind old man with the long white beard, but went back to say sorry. That reminded us of the parable of the two sons and the loving father, which Jesus told.

The next gem to appear was the green emerald, when Cassandra stopped to help her worst enemy, Cruella. That reminded us of the parable of the good Samaritan.

After that, the blue sapphire appeared on the crown, when

Cassandra gave golden badges to all the animals who'd helped her get past the wall, even though some of them had fallen asleep for most of the time. That reminded us of the parable of the workers in the vineyard.

Then it was the purple amethyst that appeared, when Cassandra used the precious golden recorder to play some music instead of keeping it hidden in her bag. That reminded us of the parable of the three servants.

Last of all, the shining pearl appeared as well. That was when Cassandra was prepared to give everything she had, even her whole life, to get past the giant. It reminded us of the parable of the valuable pearl, which Jesus told to his disciples. Just like all the parables, he was trying to tell them about the secrets of the kingdom of heaven.

Do you remember, Cassandra has been trying to find out the secret of the crown? She knew it was something to do with the gems that kept appearing on the crown, but she wasn't sure what the secret actually was. She was about to ask the kind old man for help when the little elf with the squeaky voice jumped with excitement and pointed at the crown again. 'Look, look!' he shouted. 'Look at the crown!' Just then, the five gems all started moving around on the crown, twisting and turning and changing places. *(Move the gems so that they end up spelling 'Jesus'.)* Finally, they stopped moving and Cassandra stared in amazement. 'This crown belongs to Jesus,' she said in an awestruck voice. 'Only a king has a crown, so Jesus must be a king! And a king has a kingdom, of course!'

Cassandra was right. Jesus is a king, a very special kind of king. His kingdom is the kingdom of heaven, and Jesus explained all about his kingdom using the parables, which we can find in the Bible. That's why it says in the Bible, 'Jesus said, "I have explained the secrets about the kingdom of heaven to you."' If we understand the parables that Jesus told, we can start to understand about the kingdom of heaven.

At last the little elf said to Cassandra, 'You've done it! You've actually learnt the secret of the crown!' Cassandra was so pleased, and she felt the warm glow deep inside her again, except this time it was warmer than ever. Everything felt perfect. The kind old man with the long white beard was smiling happily and the little elf was jumping up and down with excitement.

Just then, the cave started swirling all around Cassandra and there was a funny rushing noise, although she felt quite safe. *(The five gems should be removed from the crown while the swirling movement happens.)* When the noise stopped, Cassandra realised that she was back in the spare room in her house. There were dusty boxes everywhere and everything was still. She had the crown in her hands but all the gems had disappeared, Carefully, she tried putting it back on her head again, but nothing happened this time so she put it back into its box. She wondered if it had all been a dream, but somehow she knew it was real.

The story of Cassandra and the crown is a story about something very real indeed. It's a story about what it's like when Jesus is king and people live in his kingdom. That's why the gems spelt out 'Jesus', to remind us of who Christians believe is the true king. The gems reminded us about what people must be like in Jesus' kingdom. We must turn back to God and say 'sorry' when things go wrong. We must love everyone, even our worst enemies. We must remember that everyone is equally special to God. We must remember that God gives us our lives and we must use our talents well. And we must remember that God's kingdom is more important than anything else, so we must be prepared to give everything to find our place there.

Those are the secrets of the kingdom of heaven. If we've really learnt that, we know what it means to say Jesus is our king. I wonder if you'll remember what the secret of the crown was and what the gems all meant. And I wonder if you'll remember about the secrets of the kingdom of heaven. I wonder.

Cassandra's crown:
Ideas for classroom follow-up

Alongside the main weekly assembly, you can develop the themes of the story in your classroom. One or more of the following ideas could be used.

- The parables listed above can be explored fully and in more detail. Modern retellings can also be included. Role-play, hot-seating and freeze-frame drama strategies are all possibilities. It would be good to create images (poster or computer) to represent the meanings of the parables—for example, a collage of words and pictures to illustrate the talents of people in the class.
- Stories with parallel meanings or challenges can be used. For example, consider the wisdom of the actions of Daniel and Jason Rodd, who used their body boards to save the lives of three adults in difficulty in the sea (see www.prideofbritain.com/contentpages/winners/2006/daniel-jason.aspx).

  Discuss whether it can sometimes be unwise for children to go to the aid of people in trouble, and think about the best ways of helping.
- The values associated with the story (love and honesty) can be explored in a variety of contexts. You could talk about different types of love—for example, the love of music, food, pets, family members and friends.
- A recurring theme throughout the story is Cassandra's persistence and her willingness to try hard. This could link with New Year's resolutions at the start of the term.

Within the curriculum, you could make links with science, art, geography, literacy, PSHE, Citizenship, history and RE. You can find ideas on the website, www.barnabasinschools.org.uk/schools6993.

*

Section Four

The humility of Jesus

Key Bible verse

Christ was humble. He obeyed God and even died on a cross.
PHILIPPIANS 2:8

Values

Humility and hope

This section is designed to run from after the February break until Easter. The theme is the obedience of Jesus, and in the big story of God's love for the world we are remembering the way in which Jesus was very different from other leaders. When we imagine ourselves within this part of the story, we discover what it means to be humble and how this helps us come close to God.

The story of the witness birds is told in six parts as an illustration of the biblical accounts of the death and resurrection of Jesus. These are found in the Gospels.

- Week 1: Palm Sunday (Luke 19:29–40)
- Week 2: The last supper (John 13:3–16)
- Week 3: Arrest in the garden of Gethsemane (Luke 22:39–53)
- Week 4: Jesus before Pontius Pilate and Peter's denial (John 18:25—19:7)
- Week 5: Jesus is mocked (Luke 23:32–43)
- Week 6: Jesus is crucified (Luke 23:44–49)

The storyteller's prop consists of:

- Five A4-sized pictures of the witness birds (see pages 211–215 for templates), coloured in, laminated and with a central hole made at the top of each, using a hole-punch;
- A wooden perch with five nails, which turns into a cross (see pages 216–217 for details)

Line drawings of the five birds and a photograph of an example of the prop can be found on the website, www.barnabasinschools.org.uk/schools6993.

Suggested music

Suggestions for pre-recorded music that could be used at the start and end of assemblies include:

- *St Matthew Passion* (J.S. Bach, Naxos BIS-SACD–1500)
- *Miserere* (Allegri, Naxos 8.553238)
- *Canon in D* (J. Pachelbel, Naxos 8.550521)

Suggestions for songs that could be sung at assemblies include:

- A new commandment (Week Two) (SoF 22)
- Do not be afraid, for I have redeemed you (Week Five) (HO&N 111)
- From heav'n you came (Weeks Three and Four) (SoF 120)
- Hosanna, hosanna, hosanna in the highest (Week One) (SoF 189)
- In the upper room (Week Two) (TCH 117)
- Jesus, remember me when you come into your kingdom (Week Six) (HO&N 276)
- Make me a channel of your peace (Week Three) (JP 161)
- Meekness and majesty (Weeks Four and Five) (SoF 390)

- Peace, perfect peace, is the gift of Christ our Lord (Week Three) (HO&N 414)
- There is a green hill (Week Six) (JP 245)
- We have a king who rides a donkey (Week One) (JP 264)
- When we walk with the Lord (Weeks Four and Five) (SoF 599)

*

The witness birds: Week One

Bible link

This week's Bible passage link is Luke 19:29–40, which recounts the day Jesus entered Jerusalem on a donkey, when the people waved palms to welcome him.

Key theme

This week's key theme is 'being popular'. When Jesus rode into Jerusalem, it was to the acclaim of the crowds. They hoped he would be the Messiah they were waiting for. Discussion can focus on experiences of being popular or unpopular, ways in which we show regard for others and so on.

Episode One

I wonder if you enjoy listening to the birds singing as they start to make their nests. Maybe you have a favourite bird of your own. Today I want to start telling you a story about five extraordinary birds. It's a very special story, because it tells us things about God and Jesus, and it reminds us of something very important that's in the Bible.

These five extraordinary birds never seem to get old and, during their long lives, they've seen so many things! They like to sit around and tell one another all about them, and that's why they're called the witness birds. Here they are now. *(Use the 'perch' with nails to hang the bird pictures on, one by one, introducing them as they appear: sparrow, dove, owl, cockerel and crow.)*

One day, the five witness birds were together and the other four asked the sparrow to tell them about the things he'd seen. *(Take the sparrow off his nail and hold him up.)* So the sparrow started talking. 'I've witnessed some amazing things in my life. One time I flew all the way to Iceland, which is an island near the North Pole. There was snow everywhere, but they have water spouts shooting up from under the ground and they have hot water pools. In fact, they have volcanoes as well and, on 15 November 1963 when I was there, a whole new island was made when an under-water volcano erupted!'

The other four birds were impressed, but the sparrow kept on talking. 'And that reminds me of something else I once saw. I was at the funfair and the crazy rides were just like volcanoes! They went up and down so high and they were very noisy. There were stalls selling candyfloss and there were horses you could ride on.' *(The event that the sparrow witnessed should reflect one familiar to the children, but the link to the next of the sparrow's memories needs to be horses.)*

The other four birds were very impressed, but the sparrow still kept on talking. 'And that reminds me of something else I once saw. In the year 1066, I actually saw William the Conqueror sail over the English Channel from Normandy in France and invade England. He had lots of men with him and they all landed from the boats, but King Harold marched his army to meet William and there was a big battle at Hastings. I was really there, perched on a tree!' The other birds were amazed, but the sparrow kept on talking. 'William won the battle and he rode to London on a big horse, bigger than any of the horses at the funfair I told you about. When he arrived, he was crowned King of England on Christmas Day.'

The other four birds were even more impressed at what the sparrow had seen, but still he kept talking. 'And that reminds me of something else I once saw. About 2000 years ago I saw a man called Jesus. He'd spent three years telling people about the kingdom of God and now he was going to a city called Jerusalem. Everyone thought he would become the king, just like William the Conqueror a thousand years later. William defeated his enemies, but Jesus said to everyone that we should love our enemies. If you ask me, that was a big mistake! And William wore special clothes and dressed like a king to look different, but Jesus was dressed the same as everyone else. If you ask me, that was a big mistake! And William rode on a massive horse, but Jesus rode on a donkey into Jerusalem. If you ask me, that was a big mistake! That's far too humble! If only he'd found a proper horse, then, like William the Conqueror, he could have crushed all his enemies and ruled for a long time. Jesus could have been just like that—but he didn't crush his enemies, he didn't put on special clothes, and he didn't ride on a proper king's horse, just on a donkey. If you ask me, he was just too humble for his own good.'

Then the sparrow stopped talking and the five birds fell silent. *(Replace the sparrow on his nail.)* They were all feeling sad, but then the sparrow looked around at the other birds. 'Do you remember that other time when we were all together and we were watching the apostle Paul write one of his letters?' said the sparrow excitedly. 'Oh yes,' said the other birds. 'It was when he was writing to the Philippians.' The sparrow thought very hard for a moment or two and then he remembered what Paul had written: 'Christ was humble. He obeyed God and even died on a cross.' 'I wonder why Jesus had to be so humble,' said the sparrow. But the birds couldn't understand why.

That's all I've got time to tell you about the five witness birds today. I'll tell you some more next time, but wouldn't it have been amazing to have witnessed all those things the sparrow saw? I wonder what it was like to see a new island being made near Iceland and to see William the Conqueror arrive in London on a big horse. And I wonder what it was like to see Jesus arrive in Jerusalem on a donkey. I wonder why he was so humble. I wonder.

Suggested prayer

Heavenly Father, we thank you for stories and for the story of the five witness birds. Help us to remember what the sparrow saw and help us to understand why Jesus wasn't like other kings. We know that Jesus was so humble that he rode on a donkey. Help us to be humble, too, so that we can be like him. Amen

The witness birds: Week Two

Bible link

This week's Bible passage link is John 13:3–16, which recounts the events of the last supper, when Jesus washed the feet of his disciples.

Key theme

This week's key theme is 'serving others'. At the last supper Jesus washed the feet of his disciples. He demonstrated the idea that his followers should be willing and quick to serve others. Discussion can focus on ways in which people can and do serve one another. This will enable an exploration of one of the values associated with this theme—humility.

Episode Two

(Show the perch with the five birds.) Do you remember the story we started hearing last time? Which five birds are these? Can you remember what the sparrow saw?

One day, the witness birds were talking together and the other four asked the dove to tell them about some of the things he'd seen. *(Take the dove off his nail and hold him up.)* 'I've witnessed some amazing things in my time,' he said. 'I remember one time when I saw the heaviest rainfall that's ever been recorded in history! It was on 15 March 1952 and I witnessed 1.85m of rain in 24 hours. That's as deep as a swimming pool! It happened at a place called Cilaos, on an island near Madagascar.'

The other four birds were impressed, but the dove kept on talking. 'But that wasn't as amazing as the time I saw a tornado hit the town of Keokuk, Iowa, USA, on 4 July 1995. It rained there as well and in the rain were some soft drink cans that the tornado had lifted from a cola bottling plant about 240 kilometres to the south. The cans came down in the school playground and the children drank them for lunch!'

The other four birds were very impressed, but the dove kept on talking. 'That reminds me of something else I once saw. I was sitting up on the roof at the local school and I saw all the children having their lunch. There weren't any cola cans brought by a tornado, but the children had lots of different drinks and delicious food. The children had to put their hands up when they'd finished and then they could go out to play.' *(The event that the dove witnessed should reflect dinner time at the children's school.)*

The other four birds were even more impressed, but the dove kept on talking. 'And that reminds me of something else I once saw. I was at Windsor Castle when the Queen had a banquet to celebrate her 80th birthday. I was sitting up in the rafters in the great hall. There were reports in all the papers and on TV. All her friends were invited and they used solid gold plates. The food was amazing, and whenever anyone came near the Queen they bowed their head to show how important she was. I really saw it!'

The other four birds were amazed at what the dove had seen, but still he kept talking. 'And that reminds me of something else I once saw. About 2000 years ago I saw a man called Jesus. He'd spent three years telling people about the kingdom of God, and now he was going to a city called Jerusalem. Everyone thought he would become a mighty ruler, just like the Queen nearly 2000 years later. Jesus even had a special meal with his friends, just like the Queen did in Windsor Castle. But it wasn't really the same. The Queen had gold plates and rich food in a castle, but Jesus just had an ordinary meal using ordinary plates, and it was upstairs in an ordinary room. If you ask me, that was a big mistake! And there were reports about the Queen's banquet on TV, but nobody knew about Jesus' meal. If you ask me, that was a big mistake! And do you remember how I saw everyone bowing their heads to the Queen? Well, Jesus was the opposite. He actually got down and washed the feet of his disciples, just like a servant. If you ask me, that was a big mistake!'

The other four birds were listening carefully to the dove now. 'I mean, who washes other people's feet? That's far too humble. If only he'd made all the others bow their heads to him, then he would have been a proper king. But Jesus didn't have a massive banquet in a castle with gold plates and rich food, he didn't make sure everyone knew about his special meal, and he didn't get the others to bow their heads to him—he actually washed their feet. If you ask me, he was just too humble for his own good.'

The dove stopped talking and the five birds fell silent. *(Replace the dove on his nail.)* They were feeling sad. Then the dove suddenly said, 'Do you remember the time when we were all watching the apostle Paul write one of his letters?' The other birds nodded their heads. 'It was when he was writing to the Philippians.' The dove thought hard for a moment or two and then he remembered what Paul had written: 'Christ was humble. He obeyed God and even died on a cross.' 'I wonder why Jesus had to be so humble,' said the dove. But the birds couldn't understand why.

That's all I've got time to tell you about the five witness birds today. I'll tell you some more next time, but wouldn't it have been amazing to have witnessed all those things the dove saw? I wonder what it was like to see the heaviest rainfall ever and to see cola cans fall out of the sky. I wonder what it was like to see the Queen's banquet for her 80th birthday. And I wonder what it was like to see Jesus washing the feet of his disciples. I wonder why he was so humble. I wonder.

Suggested prayer

Heavenly Father, we thank you for stories and for the story of the five witness birds. Help us to remember what the dove saw and help us to understand why Jesus wasn't like other mighty rulers. We know that Jesus was so humble that he washed the feet of his disciples. Help us to be humble, too, so that we can be like him. Amen

The witness birds: Week Three

Bible link

This week's Bible passage link is Luke 22:39–53, which recounts the arrest of Jesus in the garden of Gethsemane.

Key theme

This week's key theme is 'non-violence'. Even though it meant he had no protection, Jesus would not allow Peter to use a sword against those who came to arrest him. Discussion can focus around peaceful ways of resolving difficulties and disagreements in the playground.

Episode Three

(Show the perch with the five birds.) Do you remember our story from last time? Which five birds are these? Can you remember what the dove saw?

One day, the five witness birds were sitting around talking and the other four asked the owl to tell them about some of the things he'd seen. *(Take the owl off his nail and hold him up.)* 'Well, I've witnessed some amazing things in my time,' he said. 'I remember in 1666 there was a massive fire in London, called the Great Fire of London, and I actually saw it. It started in a baker's shop on Pudding Lane and it burnt for six whole days. Eighty-nine churches were destroyed and over 13,000 houses. It was quite a sight, I can tell you!'

The other four birds were very impressed, but the owl kept

on talking. 'And that reminds me of something else I once saw. I went to the local Bonfire Night celebrations, and they had amazing fireworks. There were rockets that shot up into the sky, and fountains that made showers of sparks, and noisy fireworks as well. And the bonfire was really big.' *(The event that the dove witnessed should reflect one familiar to the children, but the link to the next of the owl's memories needs to be Bonfire Night.)*

The other four birds were even more impressed, but the owl still kept on talking. 'And that reminds me of something else I once saw. The date was 5 November 1605 and King James the First was in London, in the Houses of Parliament. A man called Guy Fawkes was there, with some others, who wanted to blow the king up. They were his enemies! They put lots of gunpowder in the cellars and everything was ready. But the king got suspicious and sent one of his loyal friends, the Earl of Sainsbury, to find out what was going on. Guy Fawkes was captured and had all his weapons taken away. He was locked up and the king was safe again. I really saw it!'

The other four birds were amazed at what the owl had seen, but still he kept talking. 'And that reminds me of something else I once saw. About 2000 years ago I saw a man called Jesus. He'd spent three years telling people about the kingdom of God and now he was going to a city called Jerusalem. Everyone thought he would become a mighty ruler, just like King James nearly 1600 years later. One night Jesus was out in a garden called the garden of Gethsemane. His enemies wanted to destroy him, just like Guy Fawkes wanted to destroy King James. But it wasn't really the same. You see, King James sent his loyal friend, the Earl of Sainsbury, to protect him from his enemies, but Jesus actually stepped out to the front himself. He didn't let his friends, the disciples, protect him. If you ask me, that was a big mistake! And King James told the Earl of Sainsbury to attack Guy Fawkes, but when Jesus' friend, Peter, got his sword out to try to fight his enemies, Jesus made him put it away again. If you ask me, that was a big mistake! And then King James arrested Guy Fawkes and punished him, but Jesus actually let himself be arrested by his enemies. If you ask me, that was a big mistake!'

The other four birds were listening carefully to the owl now. 'I mean, who doesn't put up a fight? That's far too humble. If only Jesus had made sure his friends had lots of weapons, and let them use those weapons to fight his enemies, then he would have been a proper king. Jesus could have been just like that—but he didn't hide behind his friends for protection, he didn't fight to defend himself, and he didn't arrest his enemies. He actually let himself be arrested by them. If you ask me, he was just too humble for his own good.'

Then the owl stopped talking and the five birds fell silent for a bit. *(Replace the owl on his nail.)* They were feeling quite sad about what the owl had seen, but then the owl looked around at the other birds. 'Do you remember that other time when we were all together, and we were watching the apostle Paul write one of his letters?' said the owl. 'Oh yes,' said the other birds. 'It was when he was writing to the Philippians.' The owl thought hard for a moment or two and then he remembered what Paul had written: 'Christ was humble. He obeyed God and even died on a cross.' 'I wonder why Jesus had to be so humble,' said the owl with a sad voice. But the birds couldn't understand why.

That's all I've got time to tell you about the five witness birds today. I'll tell you some more next time, but wouldn't it have been amazing to have witnessed all those things the owl saw? I wonder what it was like to see the Great Fire of London. I wonder what it was like when Guy Fawkes was planning his gunpowder plot. And I wonder what it was like to see Jesus being arrested and not putting up a fight. I wonder why he was so humble. I wonder.

Suggested prayer

Heavenly Father, we thank you for stories and for the story of the five witness birds. Help us to remember what the owl saw and help us to understand why Jesus wasn't like other mighty kings. We know that Jesus was so humble that he didn't let his friends fight to protect him. Help us to be humble, too, so that we can be like him. Amen

The witness birds: Week Four

Bible link

This week's Bible passage link is John 18:25—19:7, which recounts the trial of Jesus before Pontius Pilate and Peter's denial.

Key theme

This week's key theme is 'betrayal'. After Jesus was arrested, Peter denied knowing Jesus. This was probably because he was afraid about what might happen to him if people knew he was a friend of Jesus. Discussion can focus on ways in which people sometimes let their friends down, how hard it is sometimes not to do this, and how it feels to be let down and to know we have let someone else down.

Episode Four

(Show the perch with the five birds.) Do you remember our story from last time? Which five birds are these? Can you remember what the owl saw?

The witness birds were still talking together and the other four asked the cockerel to tell them about some of the things he'd seen. *(Take the cockerel off his nail and hold him up.)* 'I've witnessed some amazing things in my time,' he said. 'I remember on the night of 6 February 1933 I was on a US Navy ship called the *Ramapo*. A hurricane was blowing at 125 kilometres per hour and, suddenly, a huge wave hit the boat. It was 34 metres high, the height of 20 human grown-ups piled up on top of one another. It was the highest wave ever recorded!'

The other four birds were very impressed, but the cockerel kept on talking. 'And that reminds me of something else I once saw. I was at the local swimming pool and all the children were having a swim and a play. It was just like a storm! The children were splashing each other and making waves as big as they could. I was really frightened!' *(The event that the dove witnessed should reflect one familiar to the children.)*

The other four birds were even more impressed, but the cockerel still kept on talking. 'And that reminds me of another storm I once saw. A long time ago, in the year 1189, King Richard the Lionheart became King of England. He went off on the Crusades and won a great battle at a place called Arsuf in 1191, but then he decided to go back to England on a ship. There was a big storm and his ship was driven into a port called Venice, in Italy. He was captured by some enemies and taken before the Emperor. First of all, King Richard tried to pretend he wasn't really the king at all, but when they recognised him, he boasted about how important he was. In the end his friends had to collect 34 tonnes of gold to pay for him to be released. I really saw it all!'

The other four birds were amazed at what the cockerel had seen, but still he kept talking. 'And that reminds me of something else I once saw. About 2000 years ago I saw a man called Jesus. He'd spent three years telling people about the kingdom of God and now he was going to a city called Jerusalem. Everyone thought he would become a mighty ruler, just like King Richard the Lionheart nearly 1200 years later. After Jesus was arrested, he was brought before the Roman Governor, called Pontius Pilate, just like King Richard was brought before the Emperor.

But it wasn't the same. Richard the Lionheart denied he was a king to start with, but Jesus didn't deny that he was a king at all. If you ask me, that was a big mistake! And then Richard started boasting about how important he was, but Jesus didn't do that. He just said that his kingdom didn't belong to this world. If you ask me, that was a big mistake! And then, finally, King Richard got his friends to pay all that gold to get him released, but Jesus didn't try to get anyone to pay for him to be released. He humbly accepted punishment even though he didn't deserve it. In fact, Jesus' friend Peter denied that he even knew him! I actually saw it and it says in the Bible that a cockerel crowed when it happened. But if you ask me, it was all a big mistake!'

The other four birds were listening carefully to the cockerel now. 'A proper king uses cunning and power and money to escape from trouble. Why didn't Jesus just tell a lie and get himself out of trouble, like King Richard tried to do? Or why didn't Jesus boast about how important he was, like King Richard did? Or why didn't Jesus get his friends to collect up lots of money and pay for him to be released, like King Richard did? If you ask me, Jesus was too humble for his own good.'

The cockerel stopped talking and the five birds fell silent. *(Replace the cockerel on his nail.)* They were feeling sad. Then the cockerel said, 'Do you remember the time when we were all watching the apostle Paul write one of his letters, to the Philippians?' He thought hard for a moment and then he remembered what Paul had written: 'Christ was humble. He obeyed God and even died on a cross.' 'I wonder why Jesus had to be so humble,' said the cockerel. But the birds couldn't understand why.

That's all I've got time to tell you about the five witness birds today. I'll tell you some more next time, but wouldn't it have been amazing to have witnessed all those things the cockerel saw? I wonder what it was like to see the biggest wave in history. I wonder what it was like to see King Richard the Lionheart fight his battle, get captured and be brought before the Emperor, and have all that gold paid to set him free. And I wonder what it was like to see Jesus being brought before the Roman Governor, Pontius Pilate. I wonder why he was so humble. I wonder.

Suggested prayer

Heavenly Father, we thank you for stories and for the story of the five witness birds. Help us to remember what the cockerel saw and help us to understand why Jesus wasn't like other mighty kings. We know that Jesus was so humble that he accepted punishment, even though he didn't deserve it. Help us to be humble, too, so that we can be like him. Amen

The witness birds: Week Five

Bible link

This week's Bible passage link is Luke 23:32–43, which recounts the way in which Jesus was mocked by others.

Key theme

This week's key theme is 'bullying and persecution'. Jesus had been arrested and the crowd had turned against him. Not only that, but he was also mocked and humiliated. Discussion can focus on how people bully and taunt people today, why they do it and how it makes others feel. Consideration can also be given to ways in which teachers and pupils can ensure that these kinds of behaviour do not occur in school.

Episode Five

(Show the perch with the five birds.) Do you remember our story from last time? Which five birds are these? Can you remember what the cockerel saw?

The five witness birds were still talking together and the other four asked the crow to tell them about some of the things he'd seen. *(Take the crow off his nail and hold him up.)* 'I've witnessed some amazing things in my time,' he said. 'I remember the 1923 FA Cup Final between Bolton Wanderers and West Ham United. I saw the whole game from one of the towers. Officially, there were 126,000 people there, but I counted about 200,000. It was the biggest crowd ever at an FA Cup Final and the game kicked off 44 minutes late. The players couldn't even get into the changing rooms at half-time because of the crowds, so they stayed out on the pitch. And there was a policeman on a big white horse who had to go on to the pitch to keep people back. It was an amazing game and Bolton won it in the end, 2–0.'

The other four birds were very impressed, but the crow kept on talking. 'And that reminds me of something else I once saw. I was perched on the fence at the school and I saw some amazing games happening in the playground. Some of the children were playing netball, some were playing football, and there were other games too. It was very exciting, especially when the match was close. In fact, the children got so excited that it was almost like a battle.' (*The playground that the crow witnessed should be the one at the children's school, and the link to the next of the crow's memories needs to be a 'battle'.*)

The other four birds were even more impressed, but the crow still kept on talking. 'And that reminds me of something else I once saw. A long time ago, in the year 1625, King Charles I became King of England. But his enemies, led by a man called Oliver Cromwell, fought against him. One of the battles, which was even fiercer than in the school playground, was at a place called Newbury. There were men on horseback, men with long pikes and men with guns. In the end, King Charles was defeated. When he was captured, his enemies treated him with respect and let him stay in a nice castle, called Hurst Castle. They let him keep all his clothes and other things. But the King still cursed his enemies and said that everyone should carry on fighting against Oliver Cromwell. I saw it all!'

The other four birds were amazed at what the crow had seen, but still he kept talking. 'And that reminds me of something else

I once saw. About 2000 years ago I saw a man called Jesus. He'd spent three years telling people about the kingdom of God and now he was going to a city called Jerusalem. Everyone thought he would become a mighty ruler, just like King Charles did over 1600 years later. In fact, Jesus was captured by his enemies as well, but, instead of being treated with respect, like King Charles was, Jesus was made to wear a crown of thorns, so that his enemies could make fun of him. And King Charles was allowed to keep all his clothes, but Jesus had all his clothes ripped off him and stolen. And King Charles cursed his enemies and swore that they would pay for their evil deeds, but Jesus didn't do that. He even prayed for his enemies, the people who wanted to kill him! If you ask me, that was a big mistake!'

The other four birds were listening carefully to the crow now and he kept on talking. 'I mean, what kind of king wears a crown of thorns? And what kind of king has all his clothes and everything taken away? No, a proper king, like King Charles I all those years later, insists on keeping his dignity. Even though he'd been captured and sentenced to death, King Charles kept all his clothes. He told the people who'd captured him how bad they were and how he'd get his revenge. But Jesus wasn't like that. He didn't curse his enemies—he prayed for them. If you ask me, he was just too humble for his own good.'

Then the crow stopped talking and the five birds fell silent. *(Replace the crow on his nail.)* They were feeling very sad. Then the crow said, 'Do you remember that other time when we were all together, watching the apostle Paul writing to the Philippians? He wrote: "Christ was humble. He obeyed God and even died on a cross." I wonder why Jesus had to be so humble.' But the birds couldn't understand why.

That's all I've got time to tell you about the five witness birds today. I'll tell you some more next time. But wouldn't it have been amazing to have witnessed all those things the crow saw? I wonder what it was like to see that FA Cup Final with such a massive crowd. I wonder what it was like to see King Charles fighting a battle against Oliver Cromwell and being captured. And I wonder what it was like seeing Jesus being mocked and losing his clothes, but still praying for his enemies. I wonder why he was so humble. I wonder.

Suggested prayer

Heavenly Father, we thank you for stories and for the story of the five witness birds. Help us to remember what the crow saw and help us to understand why Jesus wasn't like other mighty kings. We know that Jesus was so humble that he accepted the mockery of his enemies and even prayed for them. Help us to be humble, too, so that we can be like him. Amen

The witness birds: Week Six

Bible link

This week's Bible passage link is Luke 23:44–49, which recounts the crucifixion of Jesus.

Key theme

This week's key theme is 'different perceptions'. The two men crucified alongside Jesus had very different responses to him. The people around him had various ideas about who he was. Discussion can focus around how everyone creates different impressions of themselves in different contexts. Pupils can reflect on how they would like people to remember them when they leave the school.

Episode Six

(*Show the perch with the five birds.*) Do you remember our story from last time? Which five birds are these? Can you remember what the five different birds saw? Do you remember about the sparrow seeing William the Conqueror arriving in London on a huge horse? Do you remember about the dove seeing the banquet for the Queen's 80th birthday? Do you remember about the owl seeing King James almost getting blown up by Guy Fawkes? Do you remember about the cockerel seeing Richard the Lionheart being captured? And do you remember about the crow seeing King Charles curse his enemies?

The five witness birds were still all sitting together, talking about the different things they'd seen throughout history. Before long they were talking about the different things they'd seen Jesus do. The sparrow remembered seeing Jesus arrive in Jerusalem on a donkey. The dove remembered seeing Jesus serve his disciples and wash their feet. The owl remembered seeing Jesus refuse to put up a fight when he was arrested. The cockerel remembered seeing Jesus abandoned by his friends. And the crow remembered seeing Jesus being mocked and persecuted.

They couldn't understand why Jesus had been so humble and unlike the other mighty rulers. Surely it was all a big mistake?

The witness birds fell silent. Then the sparrow chirped up softly, 'But do you remember what happened next? It was even worse than anything that had happened before. We all saw it, and we were so frightened, we flew away and tried to hide. We lost all hope.' *(Take the birds off their nails and let them fall to the floor.)*

The five birds remembered the scene so clearly, it was as if they could see it all happening in front of their eyes. Jesus was taken to a hill outside Jerusalem and he was nailed to a cross by some soldiers. *(Turn the perch into a cross with nails by swivelling the shorter piece of wood on the pivot, and hold it up high.)* The nails were very sharp and painful. A sign was made saying that Jesus was a king, and it was put up above him. Next to Jesus, two other men were nailed to crosses as well. They could see the sign above Jesus. One of the men kept cursing Jesus and saying, 'Aren't you a proper king? Why can't you save us?' But the other man just said, 'Jesus, remember me when you're ruling over your kingdom.' Jesus said to him, 'Today, you will be with me in paradise.'

The five birds were watching from nearby, trying to keep

hidden. They couldn't understand what was happening. 'What kind of king is so humble?' they asked each other. All that humility had led nowhere. It was such a waste. They felt like joining in with the man on the other cross, who cursed Jesus and said, 'Why aren't you a proper king? Why can't you save yourself?'

The sparrow looked around at the other birds. 'Do you remember that other time when we were all together, and we were watching Paul write one of his letters?' he said. 'What did he write? I can't quite remember.' The birds were all so sad and puzzled, it took them a long time to remember what Paul had written, but in the end they managed. 'Christ was humble. He obeyed God and even died on a cross.' 'I wonder why he had to be so humble,' said the sparrow. 'I wonder why he had to be nailed to a cross like that.' But the birds still couldn't understand why.

Just then, the five birds heard a little noise behind them. They looked round and were very surprised to see a tiny robin perched nearby. 'Why are you all here, looking at this cross?' the robin said to them. The witness birds began to explain everything they'd seen. The sparrow said how he'd seen Jesus arrive in Jerusalem on a donkey. The dove said how he'd seen Jesus serve his disciples and wash their feet. The owl said how he'd seen Jesus refuse to put up a fight when he was arrested. The cockerel said how he'd seen Jesus being abandoned by his friends. And the crow said how he'd seen Jesus being mocked and persecuted. Then they all said how they'd seen Jesus being nailed to the cross. 'But still he prayed for his enemies,' said the crow. 'We can't understand what Jesus was doing. We can't understand what kind of king he was. If you ask us, he made a big mistake.'

The robin was quiet for a moment as he stared up at the cross. A little tear rolled down from his eye. Then he looked back at the five frightened and worried witness birds, still trying to hide. 'I can tell you why Jesus did all those things,' he said. 'It wasn't a mistake. I can explain everything.'

I haven't got time today to tell you what the robin said to the witness birds. Next time I'll tell you the rest of the story, because it's nearly finished now. But I wonder what it would have been like to be with the witness birds, seeing Jesus on the cross? Would we have been frightened, like them? I wonder why people put a sign above Jesus, saying he was a king. I wonder why Paul wrote, 'Christ was humble. He obeyed God and even died on a cross.' I wonder.

Suggested prayer

Heavenly Father, we thank you for stories and for the story of the five witness birds. Help us to remember what the birds saw and help us to understand why Jesus wasn't like other mighty kings. We know that Jesus was so humble that he was treated like a poor criminal and, even when he was suffering, he cared for others. Help us to be humble, too, so that we can care like him. Amen

The witness birds:
Concluding celebration

The story of the witness birds is designed to end with a Holy Week or Easter celebration. You could plan a celebration using palm crosses. The concluding episode of the story reminds us how Christians believe that, even though he suffered, Jesus makes possible the hope of coming close to God.

Concluding episode

Do you remember the five witness birds? (*Show the five bird pictures one by one, not on the perch.*) Do you remember the sparrow, the dove, the owl, the cockerel and the crow? They've seen so many things from history and they've seen Jesus do so many things as well. But one thing made them very frightened, so that they had to fly away and hide. (*Show the wooden cross with nails.*) They saw Jesus being nailed to a cross. The witness birds couldn't understand what kind of king Jesus was and they couldn't understand why the apostle Paul wrote, 'Christ was humble. He obeyed God and even died on a cross.' They were thinking that Jesus must have made a big mistake.

But do you remember the little robin? He'd found the five witness birds looking up at the cross, and asked them why they were so sad and puzzled. So the robin promised to try to explain everything to them.

'Imagine there was a lovely garden,' began the robin. 'It had beautiful rich, red earth and strong fences and the sun shone down. The garden was filled with green plants and wonderful flowers. In fact, it was the perfect place to live. But imagine that something went wrong and the garden was completely flooded.' A tear rolled down the robin's face as he went on explaining, and the witness birds listened carefully. 'The garden was in a mess—and that's what the world is like as well. It's such a beautiful place but it's a sad place as well, whenever people argue or do nasty things.' The witness birds looked at one another sadly. They knew the robin was telling the truth. They'd seen so many sad things happen throughout history, even though the world was such a beautiful place to live in.

The robin started talking again. 'I suppose we could just say that there's nothing anyone can do about it. We could just say that the sad things will always happen and we have to put up with them. That would be like leaving the garden all flooded for ever and trying to grow plants even though it's very difficult. But we mustn't be like that!

'Or I suppose we could get angry about the sad things and stop caring about the world altogether. That would be like destroying the garden, so that it became a wilderness. But we mustn't be like that, either!' The witness birds all shook their heads sadly. They knew that sometimes people did destroy the beauty of the earth.

'There is one other thing that can help,' said the robin. 'People who follow Jesus believe that we must trust in him and trust in what he did when he was nailed to the cross.' The witness birds looked up at the cross. They still didn't understand. They still thought Jesus had made a big mistake. Then the robin asked them, 'What did the apostle Paul write about Jesus and the cross?' The witness birds whispered to each other and then the crow answered, 'Christ was humble. He obeyed God and even died on a cross.'

'Yes!' said the robin. 'That's right. Christians call Jesus "Christ" to show that he was God. Jesus humbled himself when he became a man. God could have said he didn't care any more about his creation, but he did still care about it. He cared so much he sent his only Son, Jesus, who humbled himself and became like one of us here on earth.' The witness birds began to nod their heads as they listened to the robin.

'Jesus was always obedient to God,' continued the robin. 'He did everything God wanted him to, even when it was very difficult and dangerous. He didn't get angry and start fighting for himself. He even accepted death on the cross of nails. But it wasn't a big mistake. It wasn't a mistake at all. In fact, it was the only way of showing how much God loved the world.'

Just then, the robin pointed up at the cross again. *(Turn the cross around.)* The witness birds gasped with surprise. 'Look at the cross!' they shouted. 'The nails are gone! Jesus is alive!'

'Now do you understand?' said the robin with a laugh. 'Jesus couldn't be like all those other mighty kings and queens. They couldn't sort out all the sad things in the world, just as the one who was supposed to look after the beautiful garden couldn't make the flood go away. The plants seemed to die, but the seeds that were buried grew into new plants when the flood ended. Jesus had to humble himself and die on the cross so that he could receive new life. You thought it was a big mistake, but in fact it was our only hope.'

The five witness birds all looked at one another. They had seen so many amazing things throughout history in their lives. They'd seen volcanoes, giant waves, big fires, massive crowds, lots of things at school and all sorts of kings and queens. But now they realised they had all witnessed the most important thing that had ever happened in history. They had witnessed Jesus being humble, dying on a cross and rising to new life again. They had seen the thing that brings hope. They had seen the only thing that makes sure God and his creation can be joined together again.

*

The witness birds:
Ideas for classroom follow-up

Alongside the main weekly assembly, you can develop the themes of the story in your classroom. One or more of the following ideas could be used.

- The narratives of Holy Week can be explored fully and in detail using the Bible references on page xx. Resources are also available on collective worship websites and in a wide range of books.
  - www.cowo.culham.ac.uk/multimedia/050x_easter.php gives a PowerPoint presentation of Easter
  - www.cowo.culham.ac.uk/assemblies/011p_palmsunday.php gives an act of worship for Palm Sunday
  - *The Life of Jesus through the Eyes of an Artist: Teacher's Guide* by David Barton with Jo Fageant (Barnabas, 2004) retells the story, and an accompanying CD ROM provides pictures.
  - *Eyewitness Assemblies* by Gaynor Cobb (Barnabas, 2007) also offers some good ideas designed for use with KS2;
  - *Beyond the Candle Flame* by Brian Ogden and Jo Dobbs (Barnabas, 2006) gives appropriate worship suggestions for Key Stage 1.
- Explore the narrative through the Stations of the Cross. www.cptryon.org/prayer/child/stations/index.html gives a child-friendly and thought-provoking version and a Google image search will provide alternative representations.
- Explore the narratives of Holy Week through art. A web search provides plenty of images.
- Explore different representations of the cross and their meanings and significance. *A-Cross the World* by Martyn Payne and Betty Pedley (Barnabas, 2004) is an excellent resource for this project.

- Link the theme of new life, together with hope, with the Easter narrative. Images of spring will support this theme. An Easter garden could be created as a visual focus for the end of the story.

There are a great many references to historical events, places in the world and features of the planet and its weather system that enable some history and geography links with the witness birds story. There are also possible curriculum links with science, art, literacy and RE. You can find ideas on the website www.barnabasinschools. org.uk/schools6993.

*

Section Five

Jesus: risen and ascended

Key Bible verse
A seed must die before it can sprout from the ground.
1 CORINTHIANS 15:36

Values
Peace and understanding

This section is designed to run from after the Easter holiday until the May break. The theme is 'Jesus: risen and ascended', and in the big story of God's love for the world we are remembering that, although Jesus is not with us, he still sends the Holy Spirit to help us. When we imagine ourselves within this part of the story, we discover how God gives us the chance to live life to the full.

The story of the amazing flowerpot is told in six parts as an illustration of the resurrection appearances of Jesus, his ascension and the gift of the Holy Spirit at Pentecost. These accounts are found in the Gospels.

- Week 1: Matthew 16:21–26
- Week 2: John 20:11–18
- Week 3: Luke 24:13–35
- Week 4: John 21:1–8 and Luke 5:1–11
- Week 5: John 20:24–29
- Week 6: Matthew 28:16–20

The storyteller's prop consists of:

- A plastic flowerpot, about 30cm tall
- An imitation packet of seeds, with six seeds in it
- Six imitation plants
- Some strong perfume
- A grape
- A whistle

The imitation packet of seeds can be as simple as a small, see-through plastic bag with the words 'surprise seeds' written on it. The six seeds have the following shapes and colours and should be large enough to be clearly visible in the packet:

- A long thin green seed
- A big fat red seed
- A curly yellow seed
- A bulgy blue seed
- A white seed, round and flat
- A black seed, round and flat

The six plants have different characteristics but can all be made using a suitable green wooden gardening stick for the stalk (except the sixth flower).

- First flower: a plain green flower made from sponge material
- Second flower: a fairly plain yellow flower made from tissue paper, with the grape attached
- Third flower: a larger bright multicoloured flower made from tissue paper
- Fourth flower: a suitably textured 'feely' flower, possibly made from a dusting glove
- Fifth flower: a red trumpet-shaped flower made from craft paper
- Sixth flower: a flower-shaped helium balloon, for which the string acts as the stalk

The perfume is used with the first flower. The whistle is used with the fifth flower. The flowerpot should be prepared so that the flowers can stand within it easily. A photograph of an example prop can be found on the website, www.barnabasinschools.org. uk/schools6993.

Suggested music

Suggestions for pre-recorded music that could be used at the start and end of the assemblies include:

- Hallelujah Chorus from *Messiah* (G.F. Handel, Naxos 8.553258)
- Theme tune from a TV gardening programme

Suggestions for songs that could be sung at the assemblies include:

- A butterfly, an Easter egg (TCH 1)
- Colours of day (JP 28)
- Come on and celebrate (SoF 73)
- God's not dead (JP 60)
- Lord, the light of your love is shining (SoF 362)
- Morning has broken (JP 166)
- Rejoice in the Lord always (JP 208)
- This is the day (JP 255)

*

The amazing flowerpot: Week One

Bible link

This week's Bible passage link is Matthew 16:21–26, in which Jesus tells his disciples that he will have to die in order to find true life.

Key theme

This week's key theme is 'feeling low and disappointment'. After Jesus' death and burial, his friends were probably confused, bewildered and disappointed. Discussion can focus on times when pupils have experienced such feelings—for example when a friend moved away. If it is appropriate to do so, there could also be some discussion about bereavement.

Episode One

I wonder if any of you have ever had a packet of seeds and tried planting them in a pot or in your garden. Today, I want to start telling you a new story about a man called Percy, who loved planting seeds and growing things. It's a very special story, because it tells us about God and Jesus, and about things in the Bible.

Once upon a time, there was a man called Percy who loved growing plants. He lived in a block of flats and didn't have a garden of his own, so he decided he would make his window ledge into a garden, because it was perfect for plant pots. Percy went to the local garden centre and he searched for a flowerpot.

(*Show the flowerpot.*) Then he took it home and filled it with earth so that it was all ready to grow plants in.

Percy had to decide what to grow in his new flowerpot. He loved carrots so he bought a packet of carrot seeds, planted them carefully in his flowerpot and then waited to see what would happen. But nothing grew at all, even though he waited a whole week. 'Maybe the earth is too dry,' thought Percy to himself. So he watered it and then went and bought a packet of tomato seeds. But none of them grew, either, although Percy was very patient. 'Maybe the earth needs extra minerals and fertiliser,' said Percy to himself. So he added a bag of special compost to the flowerpot and then he went to buy a packet of sunflower seeds. But still nothing grew at all.

By now, Percy was getting very upset about his flowerpot. Nothing seemed to grow in it at all, whatever he tried. He went back to the shop and bought a packet of seeds that said, 'Guaranteed to grow whatever the weather' on it. 'Surely these seeds will grow into something,' he said, hopefully. So he carefully sprinkled them into his flowerpot. He waited and waited, but still nothing seemed to grow.

Percy was filled with despair. He decided that nothing would ever grow in his flowerpot, so he grabbed it off the window ledge and took it back to the garden centre. 'Nothing ever grows in this flowerpot,' he said angrily to the assistant there. 'You can have it back. It's no use to me.' The assistant said, 'You mustn't ever stop trying to grow plants! I'm sure something will grow in your flowerpot. You just haven't found the right thing yet.' But Percy was determined to give the pot back. He put the pot down on the counter and was walking out of the garden centre when the assistant called to him, 'Wait a minute!

I've just remembered the perfect thing for you to try!' Percy looked round and saw that the assistant was holding up a packet of seeds. *(Show the packet of seeds.)* On it was written 'Surprise seeds'. Percy thought for a minute. Nothing had grown in his flowerpot before, but maybe it was worth one last try. On the other hand, it might just be a waste of time. He couldn't decide what to do.

In the end, Percy said to himself, 'This packet of seeds is my last hope for something to grow in my flowerpot.' He decided he would try the packet of surprise seeds, so he took the packet and the flowerpot back home. 'I wonder what will happen,' thought Percy to himself. He shook the packet and it made an interesting rattling noise, so he carefully opened it and looked inside. What he saw was very surprising.

I haven't got time now to tell you any more of my story, but I'll carry on telling it next time. In fact, it's a very special story because it reminds us about something in the Bible. One time, Jesus was talking with his disciples and told them that, when he went to Jerusalem, he would die. The disciples were very sad. They were filled with despair, just as Percy was filled with despair when all of his seeds died in the earth of his flowerpot. But Jesus told his disciples to be filled with hope, even though he would die, because he told them that death is not the end. And even Percy decided he had one last hope with the packet of surprise seeds.

The apostle Paul wrote about it in one of his letters. He wrote, 'A seed must die before it can sprout from the ground.' What he meant was that when Jesus died, he rose again. Jesus promised us that if we believe and trust him, we can be like him.

I wonder what it was like for poor old Percy to keep on trying to grow those seeds. He must have got very upset. Would we have given up in despair, like him? Would we have tried the packet of surprise seeds? Would we have tried our last hope? And I wonder what it was like to be one of the disciples, hearing Jesus say that he would die in Jerusalem. They must have been very upset and filled with despair. I wonder if they thought there was any hope left. I wonder.

Suggested prayer

Lord God, thank you for the story about Percy and his flowerpot. We know that when seeds fall into the ground, they seem to die, just like Jesus, who was buried in a tomb. Help us to remember what Paul wrote, that a seed must die before it can sprout again from the ground. Just as Percy had one last hope with the packet of surprise seeds, fill us too with hope in the resurrection of Jesus. Amen

The amazing flowerpot: Week Two

Bible link

This week's Bible passage link is John 20:11–18, which recounts the meeting of Mary Magdalene with the risen Jesus.

Key theme

This week's key theme is 'the sense of smell'. Percy's flower smelt beautiful. Not all smells are so nice, but a sense of smell is important. Consider how life might be different without it. Throughout Weeks Two to Six of the story, the idea of surprise recurs, and reflection on this could lead to discussion on pleasant and perhaps distressing surprises.

Episode Two

(Show the flowerpot and packet of seeds.) Can anyone remember the story we began last time? What was the name of the man who loved planting seeds? Did anything grow?

The story tells us something about God and Jesus. Percy was full of despair when nothing seemed to grow in his flowerpot. Can you remember what that reminds us of in the Bible?

Percy had decided to have one last go at growing something in his flowerpot, using the strange packet of 'surprise seeds'. He looked inside the packet and he saw six big seeds, different from anything he had ever seen before. There was a long thin green seed. There was a big fat red seed. There was a curly yellow seed and a bulgy blue seed. Then there was a black seed and a white seed, both round and flat.

Percy decided to plant the long thin green seed first. *('Plant' the seed in the pot.)* He was very excited and waited patiently for half an hour, watching the pot, but nothing happened. 'Maybe I need to add some water,' he said. So he added some water to the pot, but nothing happened. 'I know!' he said with a smile. 'The pot needs some fertiliser as well.' So he added some fertiliser, but still nothing happened. Percy remembered all the other packets of seeds he'd tried, none of which had grown. 'Maybe this packet of surprise seeds is just the same as the others. Maybe nothing will ever grow in my flowerpot,' he sighed to himself.

It was late by then so Percy went to bed. In the morning he rushed to the window to see if anything had grown, but nothing had happened. Percy was busy all day, and in the evening, when he looked at the flowerpot again, still nothing had grown. 'Maybe the green seed that I planted is completely dead,' he thought to himself sadly as he went to bed.

The next morning was the third day from when he'd buried the seed deep in the earth, and Percy woke up very early. The sun was shining beautifully through the curtains so Percy jumped out of bed and ran to the window to see if anything had happened in the flowerpot. What he saw amazed him. He could see a green shoot pushing up out of the earth before his very eyes. It grew and grew, getting taller and taller. Then suddenly it made an amazing flower. *(Add the plain green flower to the pot, as yet unscented.)* The whole plant was shimmering slightly. It looked very unusual, different from any plant he'd seen before. Percy wasn't sure if the flower was real, so he opened the window to get closer to it. It was shimmering, like an illusion that isn't really there, and it seemed to be very hard to get hold of. But suddenly the flower opened out a bit more and made a lovely smell. *(Release the perfume smell.)*

Percy enjoyed sniffing the air with a big smile on his face. 'Now I know this flower is real,' he said. 'Only a real plant could make such a lovely smell. I thought the seed was completely dead, but look what an amazing plant it's made!' Percy was very excited. He grabbed hold of the packet of surprise seeds and looked inside. There were still five seeds left.

I haven't got time now to tell you any more of the story, but we'll hear some more next time. It's a very special story, because it reminds us about something in the Bible. On Easter morning, the third day after Jesus had died, one of his friends, called Mary Magdalene, went to the place where he'd been buried. She was very sad, just as Percy was very sad about his seed that seemed to be completely dead. But Mary Magdalene was amazed at what happened next. The tomb where Jesus' dead body had been laid was empty. Even more amazingly, she actually met Jesus himself in the garden. He seemed to be different, just like Percy's plant was different and shimmering, and Mary wasn't quite sure if Jesus was real or not. But later on, when she told the disciples, she knew that Jesus had been completely real. It can't have been a dream, because she could remember the lovely garden smells, just as Percy could smell the lovely smell that the flower had made, so he knew that it was completely real.

Paul wrote about it in one of his letters: 'A seed must die before it can sprout from the ground.' What he meant was that when Jesus died, he rose again. Jesus promised us that if we trust him, we can be like him.

I wonder what it was like for Percy to plant that first seed in his flowerpot. He must have been full of despair when nothing seemed to happen, but I wonder how he felt on the third day when the flower with the lovely smell appeared. And I wonder how Mary Magdalene felt when she went to the tomb on Easter morning on the third day after Jesus had been buried. I expect she remembered the lovely smells in that garden, and I'm sure she remembered meeting Jesus. I wonder how we would have felt if we'd been there. I wonder.

Suggested prayer

Lord God, thank you for the story about Percy and his flowerpot. We know that when seeds fall into the ground, they seem to die, just like Jesus, who was buried in a tomb. Help us to remember what Paul wrote, that a seed must die before it can sprout again from the ground. Thank you that Mary Magdalene met the risen Jesus in the garden at Easter time and knew she wasn't dreaming because of the lovely smells there. Amen

The amazing flowerpot: Week Three

Bible link

This week's Bible passage link is Luke 24:13–35, which recounts the walk that the risen Jesus made with two of his disciples on the road to Emmaus and the meal he shared with them.

Key theme

This week's key theme is 'the sense of taste'. The fruit on Percy's flower tasted delicious. Consider the tastes that people like and dislike, as well as their favourite fruits and other foods.

Episode Three

(*Show the flowerpot and packet of seeds.*) Can anyone remember the story we're hearing? What was the name of the man who loved planting seeds? And what's special about the flower that has grown?

The story tells us something about God and Jesus. Percy could smell this flower and knew it must be real, but can you remember what that reminds us of in the Bible?

Percy looked at the five remaining seeds in the packet. He decided to plant the big fat red seed next. (*'Plant' the seed in the pot.*) 'I wonder if anything will happen with this one,' he said to himself. He watched the flowerpot carefully for a whole hour, but nothing happened. Then he remembered to add water and fertiliser, but still nothing happened. He began to wonder if only the first seed would make a plant, but by then it was getting late and Percy went to bed.

In the morning he rushed to the window to see if anything had grown, but nothing had happened. Percy had lots to do that day, and in the evening, when he looked at the flowerpot again, still nothing had grown. 'Maybe the big fat red seed that I planted is completely dead,' he thought to himself sadly. He went to bed again, very tired, wondering if anything would grow.

The next morning was the third day from when he'd buried the seed deep in the earth, and Percy woke up very early. It was another sunny day and, as he woke up, Percy remembered that he'd promised to take his friend's two dogs for a walk that morning. He could already hear them scratching at the door, so out he went and walked the dogs round the park three times. With every step he took, he became more and more sad. He was worried that nothing more would grow in the flowerpot. In the end, the two dogs were worn out so Percy rushed home to look.

He was amazed to see a little green shoot pushing up out of the earth before his very eyes. It grew and grew, getting taller and taller. Then suddenly it made a flower. *(Add the second flower with the grape to the pot.)* Percy opened the window. The whole plant was shimmering slightly and it seemed to be very hard to get hold of, but suddenly the flower opened out a bit more and Percy could see a small fruit in the middle of it. He reached out his hand, picked the fruit and popped it into his mouth. *(Pick and eat the grape.)* It was the most delicious-tasting fruit Percy had ever eaten in his whole life.

'Now I'm sure this flower is real,' said Percy. 'Only a real plant could make such a lovely-tasting fruit. I thought the second seed was completely dead, but look what an amazing plant it's made!' Percy was very excited, and he grabbed hold of the packet of surprise seeds, gave it a shake and looked inside. There were still four seeds left.

Next time we'll hear if Percy decided to plant another seed. This is a very special story, because it reminds us about something in the Bible. On Easter day, the third day after Jesus had died, two of his friends were walking from Jerusalem to a village called Emmaus. They were very sad, a bit like Percy as he walked around the park, thinking about his second seed that seemed to be completely dead. But those two disciples were amazed at what happened after that.

Someone else joined them on the road to Emmaus, and that person started explaining to them why Jesus had to die— so that God could give him new life. The disciples were very excited and when they reached Emmaus they invited the man who'd walked with them in for a meal. As they shared the bread and tasted the food, they realised that it was really Jesus who had walked with them. Suddenly he vanished. He seemed to be different, just as Percy's plant was different and shimmering, and the two disciples weren't quite sure if Jesus was real or not. But when they talked about it later, they knew that Jesus must have been completely real. They knew it couldn't have been a dream, because the bread they'd tasted was real bread, just as the fruit Percy had tasted from the flower was real.

Paul wrote about it in one of his letters: 'A seed must die before it can sprout from the ground.' What he meant was that when Jesus died, he rose again. Jesus promised us that if we trust him, we can be like him.

I wonder what it was like for Percy to plant that second seed in his flowerpot. I wonder how he felt on the third day, when the amazing plant with the flower and the fruit appeared. He must have been so excited! Would we have been the same? And I wonder how those two disciples felt when they walked with Jesus and shared a meal with him on Easter Day, on the third day after Jesus had been buried. I'm sure they remembered meeting Jesus for the rest of their lives. I wonder how we would have felt if we'd been there. I wonder.

Suggested prayer

Lord God, thank you for the story about Percy and his flowerpot. We know that when seeds fall into the ground, they seem to die, just like Jesus, who was buried in a tomb. Help us to remember what Paul wrote, that a seed must die before it can sprout again from the ground. Thank you that those two disciples met the risen Jesus on the road to Emmaus and knew they weren't dreaming because of the food they tasted with him. Amen

The amazing flowerpot: Week Four

Bible link

This week's Bible passage link is John 21:1–8 and Luke 5:1–11. These passages describe Jesus telling his disciples to cast their nets out for fish—both after the resurrection and when Jesus first asked them to follow him.

Key theme

This week's key theme is 'the sense of sight'. For Peter, seeing was believing. Consider the importance of sight and the experiences of people who live without it. Think about the support that is available for those who can't see—for example, guide dogs, the work of Louis Braille and the use of his alphabet today, and audio books and newspapers.

Episode Four

(Show the flowerpot and packet of seeds.) Can anyone remember the story we're listening to? Can you remember what's special about these two flowers that have grown?

The story tells us something about God and Jesus. Percy could smell and taste and knew the plants must be real, but can you remember what that reminds us of in the Bible?

Percy decided to plant the curly yellow seed next. *('Plant' the seed in the pot.)* He remembered to add water and fertiliser. Then he watched for hours, but nothing happened. He began to wonder if this seed would ever make a plant, but by then it was getting late and Percy went to bed. In the morning he rushed to the window to see if anything had grown, but nothing had happened. Percy was very busy that day, but in the evening, when he looked again, still nothing had grown. 'Maybe the curly yellow seed that I planted is completely dead,' he thought to himself sadly. So he went to bed, wondering if anything would have happened by the morning.

Percy slept very well that night. When he woke up the next morning it was the third day from when he'd buried the seed in the earth. The sun was just beginning to rise, and Percy was about to go and look at the flowerpot when he noticed a book next to his bed. It was a book all about flowers and plants. He turned to his favourite page and found the photograph of his favourite flower.

Percy's favourite flower was amazing. It was made of every single different colour you can think of. Percy looked at the photo for ages. Then he remembered the only time he'd ever actually seen this flower for real. It was at a big flower show, with thousands of plants on display and thousands of gardeners as well. He remembered how he'd stood and stared at this flower, his all-time favourite, for hours. He'd never forgotten that moment, but it was a long time ago now.

Then Percy remembered the flowerpot. He jumped out of bed and ran over to the window to look. What he saw amazed him. A little green shoot was pushing up out of the earth before his very eyes. It grew and grew, getting taller and taller. Then it made a big bud, ready to flower. The whole plant was shimmering slightly and Percy wasn't sure if the bud was real, so he opened the window to get closer. It was shimmering like an illusion, and it seemed to be very hard to get hold of, but suddenly the bud opened out and made an amazing flower. *(Add the third, colourful flower to the pot.)* Percy shouted with delight. It was his favourite flower, just like the one he'd seen all that time ago at the flower show! 'Now I can see with my own eyes that this flower is real,' said Percy. 'Only a real plant could make such a perfect flower, just like the one I remember. I thought that third seed might be completely dead, but look what an amazing plant it's made!' Percy was very excited, and he grabbed hold of the packet of surprise seeds, gave it a shake and looked inside. There were still three seeds left.

Next time we'll hear if Percy decided to plant another seed. This is a very special story, because it reminds us about things in the Bible. Soon after Easter day, the third day after Jesus had died, Peter and some of the other disciples were by a lake. They went fishing, but they didn't catch anything. Just then, someone on the beach shouted to them, 'Let your nets down on the right side of the boat.' So they did, and then they caught a whole net full of fish. As he looked at the fish, Peter remembered what had happened a long time ago, when he had first met Jesus. It had been the same then. They hadn't caught any fish all night, but Jesus told them to try one more time and then their nets were full. That was when Peter and the others had first started to follow Jesus, to help him bring in people instead of fish. So, as he looked at the fish, Peter knew that it was really Jesus again, just as Percy knew that the third flower was real because he'd seen it before at the flower show.

Paul wrote about it in one of his letters: 'A seed must die before it can sprout from the ground.' What he meant was that when Jesus died, he rose again. Jesus promised us that if we trust him, we can be like him.

I wonder what it was like for Percy to plant that third seed in his flowerpot and to see his favourite flower appear on the third day. He must have been so excited. Would we have been the same? And I wonder how Peter felt when he caught the fish and knew that Jesus was on the beach, soon after the third day from when Jesus had been buried. I expect he remembered all the fish he'd caught the first time, when Jesus asked him to follow him. He must have been so excited to see Jesus alive again. I wonder how we would have felt if we'd been Peter. I wonder.

Suggested prayer

Lord God, thank you for the story about Percy and his flowerpot. We know that when seeds fall into the ground, they seem to die, just like Jesus, who was buried in a tomb. Help us to remember what Paul wrote, that a seed must die before it can sprout again from the ground. Thank you that Peter saw the risen Jesus on the beach by the lake and knew he wasn't dreaming because of the fish he could see in his net. Amen

The amazing flowerpot: Week Five

Bible link

This week's Bible passage link is John 20:24–29, which tells about Thomas touching the wounds of the risen Jesus.

Key theme

This week's key theme is 'the sense of touch'. Being able to touch Jesus' wounds was what Thomas needed, to convince him that Jesus was alive. In what ways is touch used to convince people of affection or anger? Some people live with little or no sense of touch, leading to all sorts of dangers. Consider how important this sense is to people's safety.

Episode Five

(Show the flowerpot and packet of seeds.) Can anyone remember the story we're listening to? Can you remember what's special about these three flowers that have grown?

The story tells us something about God and Jesus. Percy could smell, taste and see, and so he knew that the flowers must be real, but can you remember what that reminds us of in the Bible?

It was a difficult decision but in the end Percy made up his mind to plant the bulgy blue seed next. *('Plant' the seed in the pot.)* 'I wonder if anything will happen with this one,' he said to himself. He watched the flowerpot carefully for ages, but nothing happened. Then he remembered to add water and fertiliser, but still nothing happened. He began to wonder if this seed would ever make a plant. But by then it was bedtime, and he slept all night. In the morning Percy rushed to the window to see if anything had grown, but still nothing had happened. He was out all that day, and in the evening, when he looked at the flowerpot again, nothing new had grown. 'Maybe the blue seed that I planted is completely dead,' he thought to himself sadly. So he went to bed, wondering if anything would have grown in the morning.

When Percy woke up the next morning, it was the third day from when he'd buried the seed deep in the earth. It was another sunny day and, as he woke up, Percy sat up in bed and began to think about the packet of surprise seeds. As he thought about them, he began to worry. 'Maybe they're not real after all,' he thought to himself. 'It might all be just my imagination. After all, I haven't actually touched any of the plants that have grown up in my flowerpot. Although it would be dangerous to lean out of the window too far, I don't think I'll really believe the flowers are real unless I can actually touch them.'

So Percy got out of bed and walked over to the window. He looked out on to the window ledge, and what he saw amazed him. He could see another little green shoot pushing up out of the earth before his very eyes, made by the blue seed. It grew and grew, getting taller and taller. Then suddenly it made a big and very strange flower. *(Show the fourth flower.)* The whole plant was shimmering slightly. It looked very surprising and unusual. It was completely different from any plant he'd seen before, all bumpy and peculiar. Percy remembered what he'd been thinking when he woke up. 'I won't believe it's real unless I can actually touch it,' he said, so he opened the window very carefully and began to lean out.

The window was high up, so Percy was very careful. He leaned out more and more until he could reach out with his fingers and touch the flower. It was very 'feely' and bumpy. 'Now I know that this flower is real, because I've touched it with my own hands,' said Percy. 'My flowerpot can really grow real plants. I thought the fourth seed might be completely dead, but look what an amazing plant it's made!' Percy was very excited, and he grabbed hold of the packet of surprise seeds, gave it a shake and looked inside. There were only two seeds left.

Next time we'll hear if Percy decided to plant another seed. This is a very special story, because it reminds us about things in the Bible. A week after Easter Day, the third day after Jesus had died, the disciples were together in a room. One of them was called Thomas. Now Thomas didn't believe that Jesus had risen from the dead. In fact, he said, 'First, I must see the nail scars in his hands and touch them with my finger. I must put my hand where the spear went into his side. I won't believe unless I do this!' Thomas was a bit like Percy in our story, who said he wouldn't believe that the special plants from the surprise seeds were actually real unless he could touch them. Just then, Jesus appeared to the disciples and to Thomas as well. Thomas touched Jesus and felt the wounds he'd been given when he was nailed to the cross. Then Thomas knew that Jesus really was alive—just like Percy, who reached out of his window, touched the fourth flower and then knew it was real.

Paul wrote about it in one of his letters: 'A seed must die before it can sprout from the ground.' What he meant was that when Jesus died, he rose again. Jesus promised us that if we trust him, we can be like him.

I wonder what it was like for Percy to plant that fourth seed in his flowerpot. Do you think he should have worried about whether the seeds and the plants were real? I wonder how he felt when, on the third day, he leaned out of the window and touched the fourth flower. He must have been so excited to feel such a strange plant and know it was real. And I wonder how Thomas felt when he actually touched Jesus, after all those doubts he'd had. He must have been so excited to see Jesus alive again, after everyone thought he'd died for ever. I wonder how we would have felt if we'd been Thomas. I wonder.

Suggested prayer

Lord God, thank you for the story about Percy and his flowerpot. We know that when seeds fall into the ground, they seem to die, just like Jesus, who was buried in a tomb. Help us to remember what Paul wrote, that a seed must die before it can sprout again from the ground. Thank you that Thomas could touch the risen Jesus and feel all his doubts go away. Amen

The amazing flowerpot: Week Six

Bible link

This week's Bible passage link is Matthew 28:16–20, which describes the risen Jesus telling his disciples to go out into the world and tell the good news.

Key theme

This week's key theme is 'the sense of hearing'. Hearing Jesus' voice reassured his friends. Consider what it would be like to live in a silent world. Find out about how technology, signing and lip reading can help those who experience hearing impairment. Find out about Evelyn Glennie, the world-famous percussionist. An additional theme relating to this section of the story is the idea of wanting to have a go. Percy had not played football for ages but he was willing to try. Similarly, Jesus' friends, inspired by his words, wanted to tell others about him. Discussion could focus on the importance of being willing to have a go at doing different things.

Episode Six

(*Show the flowerpot and packet of seeds.*) Can anyone remember the story we're listening to? Can you remember what's special about these four flowers that have grown?

The story tells us something about God and Jesus. Percy could smell, taste, see and touch, so he knew the flowers must be real, but can you remember what that reminds us of in the Bible?

Percy looked carefully at the two remaining seeds, the white one and the black one, both round and flat. In the end, he decided to plant the white one next. *('Plant' the seed in the pot.)* 'I wonder if anything will grow from this seed,' he said to himself. He watched the flowerpot patiently and he added water and fertiliser, but nothing happened. He began to wonder if this seed would ever make a plant, but by then it was bedtime.

In the morning he rushed to the window to see if anything had grown, but nothing had happened. Percy was out all that day, and in the evening, when he looked at the flowerpot again, still nothing had grown. 'Maybe the white seed that I planted is completely dead,' he thought to himself sadly. He went off to bed, but just as he was about to go to sleep, the phone rang. It was a friend of his, who asked Percy if he was free to play in a football match. 'I haven't played football for ages,' said Percy. 'I can't play in a match. It would be far too difficult for me. I wouldn't be good enough.' Percy's friend was very sad but nothing would persuade Percy to change his mind.

When Percy woke up the next morning, it was the third day from when he'd buried the seed deep in the earth. It was another sunny day and Percy wondered if anything had grown in the flowerpot. He jumped out of bed and ran over to the window. What he saw amazed him! He could see another little green shoot pushing up out of the earth before his eyes. It grew and grew, getting taller and taller, and then suddenly it made a very unusual flower. *(Show the fifth flower.)* The whole plant was shimmering slightly. It looked very strange, and it was completely different from any plant he'd seen before. Percy wasn't sure if it was real or not, so he opened the window very carefully to try to see. Just then, the flower made a really loud noise! (*Blow the whistle as loudly as possible.*) Percy had to cover his ears, the noise was so loud. 'Now I know that this flower is real, because I can hear it make a noise,' said Percy. 'My flowerpot can really grow real plants. I thought the fifth seed might be completely dead, but look what an amazing plant it's made!'

The noise of the whistle made Percy remember his friend and the football match. Percy grabbed the phone and called his friend straight away. 'I will play in the match!' he shouted down the phone. 'I've just heard something that's made me want to play after all!' (*Blow the whistle again.*) Then Percy picked up the packet of surprise seeds, gave it a shake and looked inside. There was only one seed left.

Next time we'll hear what happened when Percy planted the last seed. This is a very special story, because it reminds us about things in the Bible. Soon after Easter Day, the third day after Jesus had died, the disciples travelled to a mountain and Jesus met them there. They were still quite frightened and some of them weren't really sure that Jesus was alive again. They didn't feel good enough to do anything much, a bit like Percy, who didn't feel good enough to play in the football match. But then Jesus started talking to his disciples. He told them to go out into the world and tell everyone about the amazing thing that God had done when Jesus rose again. When they heard his voice, they began to think that perhaps they could do it after all. They knew that Jesus really was alive—just like Percy, who heard the noise the fifth plant made and then decided he could play in the match after all. When he heard the noise the flower made, he knew it was real.

Paul wrote about it in one of his letters: 'A seed must die before it can sprout from the ground.' What he meant was that when Jesus died, he rose again. Jesus promised us that, if we trust him, we can be like him.

I wonder what it was like for Percy to plant that fifth seed in his flowerpot. I wonder what he felt like when his friend asked him to play in the match but he didn't think he was good enough. I wonder how he felt when, on the third day, he heard the noise the fifth flower made. He must have been so excited. Would we have been the same? And I wonder how the disciples felt when they actually heard Jesus and he made them feel ready to spread the good news of what God had done. They must have been so excited to see Jesus alive again. I wonder how we would have felt if we'd been there. I wonder.

Suggested prayer

Lord God, thank you for the story about Percy and his flowerpot. We know that when seeds fall into the ground, they seem to die, just like Jesus, who was buried in a tomb. Help us to remember what Paul wrote, that a seed must die before it can sprout again from the ground. Thank you for the time when the disciples heard Jesus speak to them and were filled with bravery so that they could go and spread the good news. Amen

The amazing flowerpot: Concluding celebration

The story ends with a Pentecost celebration. You could plan a celebration using suitable songs and readings. The concluding episode reminds us how Christians believe that after Jesus had returned to be with God, he sent the Holy Spirit not only to be with his first disciples, but also to be with everyone who believes in Jesus.

Concluding episode

Do you remember the story about Percy and his amazing flowerpot, which he kept on the window ledge outside his flat? Do you remember how he almost gave up in despair when nothing grew? And do you remember the extraordinary packet of 'surprise seeds' that he was given? (*Show the packet of seeds.*) From those seeds Percy grew all sorts of plants in his flowerpot. (*Show flowerpot with five plants.*) Can you remember what's special about each of the plants?

This story reminds us about Jesus. When Jesus died, he was buried in a tomb, just as a seed is buried underground and seems to be dead. But on the third day Jesus rose again to new life, just like Percy's amazing surprise seeds, which each made a flower on the third day after he'd planted it. Paul once wrote this in one of his letters: 'A seed must die before it can sprout from the ground.' What he meant was that when Jesus died, he rose again.

To start with, Percy thought his plants might just be an illusion, but he soon discovered that they were real after all.

He smelt their scent, he tasted their fruit, he saw their colours, he touched their feely texture and he heard the noises they made. Then he knew that the plants were real. To start with, the disciples and other people thought that Jesus hadn't really risen again. They thought he was just an illusion and not real. But then they used all their senses and they knew that Jesus really was alive.

Percy still had one seed left in the packet to plant—the round flat black seed. *('Plant' the seed.)* He knew he'd have to be patient and wait for the third day for it to grow, so he added water and fertiliser to the flowerpot and he didn't worry when nothing happened straight away. Nothing grew on the second day either, but on the third morning Percy rushed to the window. He was very disappointed. However hard he looked, he couldn't see a new shoot appearing anywhere. 'Something must be wrong with the last seed,' he said to himself. 'All the others came to life on the third day.' Percy watched and waited, but nothing grew.

It was the same on the fourth and fifth days. The round flat black seed still didn't grow. As more and more days went by, Percy began to think it was hopeless. After ten days he hardly bothered checking the flowerpot at all, and after 20 days he'd almost forgotten about it altogether. Still, nothing had grown from the black seed.

When Percy woke up on the 40th day after he'd planted the seed, he decided the time had come to give up and clear the flowerpot out. He went to the window and looked at the five flowers that had grown. Percy reached for his trowel, ready to clear them away, but suddenly he stopped in amazement. A new shoot was springing up! 'It must be the last seed, after all,' laughed Percy. 'I can't believe it's taken 40 days to grow.' The shoot was very strong and it kept growing up and up, going higher and higher. *(Show the sixth flower, letting the balloon rise up steadily.)* It was the tallest plant Percy had ever seen!

It grew so high that he couldn't smell it to see if it had a nice flowery scent. He couldn't try to pick any fruit from it to taste. He couldn't see what it looked like. He couldn't touch it, and he couldn't hear if it was making any noise as it blew in the wind. But he knew it was there. 'These seeds have been very surprising,' said Percy to himself. He picked up the packet and looked on the back. This is what he read: 'If you plant these seeds you will discover something very special. You'll discover that a seed must die in the ground before it can grow up again. These seeds will tell you the true meaning of life.'

'I almost gave up gardening,' Percy said to himself, 'but these seeds have shown me some amazing things. Even the last one, which is so high it's impossible to see properly, has shown me something. I think the flower up there must be able to see the whole world. It's smiling down on everyone, not just me.' Percy was very happy.

The story of the amazing flowerpot doesn't just tell us about when Jesus rose from the dead at Easter and appeared to his disciples and to other people. The Bible says that after 40 days, Jesus went up into heaven, just like the last flower that grew in Percy's flowerpot and rose higher and higher. This last flower was so high, it was almost impossible to see, and Percy couldn't touch it. It's the same with Jesus now. We can't see him or touch him, but we know he's there. In fact, Christians believe that he can see everything and everyone now, just like the flower, which could see the whole world. Percy imagined the flower smiling on everyone and Jesus, too, smiles on everyone. Jesus promised to send his friends the gift of the Holy Spirit, which came at Pentecost, and Christians believe that he sends his special gift to us today. It is the Holy Spirit that gives Christians true life and helps them to follow Jesus in their lives.

*

The amazing flowerpot:
Ideas for classroom follow-up

Alongside the main weekly assembly, you can develop the themes of the story in your classroom. One or more of the following ideas could be used.

- The resurrection narratives can be explored fully and in detail using the relevant Bible references. Role-play, hot-seating and freeze-frame drama strategies might be used to encourage pupils to engage with the stories. Resources are also available on collective worship websites and in many books
  - www.cowo.culham.ac.uk/reflections/reflect_one.php?a598 offers a PowerPoint presentation about the ascension
  - *Beyond the Candle Flame* by Brian Ogden and Jo Dobbs (Barnabas, 2006) offers appropriate worship suggestions designed for use with KS1
  - *Eyewitness Assemblies* by Gaynor Cobb (Barnabas, 2007) includes appropriate material designed for use with KS2.
- Explore beliefs about the resurrection and the sadness that precedes it through symbolism.
  - www.cowo.culham.ac.uk/reflections/reflect_one.php?a598 offers a PowerPoint presentation about a chapel in France called the Chapel of the Resurrection
  - www.historiccoventry.co.uk/cathedrals/charredcross.php gives brief information about the Coventry Cross of Nails, a symbol of both resurrection and peace.
- Link the theme of new life, together with hope, with the resurrection narratives. Images of spring will support this theme. An Easter garden could be created as a visual focus for the end of the story.

- Explore some of the feelings experienced by the followers of Jesus during the 40 days after his resurrection—for example, hope, surprise, doubt and disbelief.

There are possible curriculum links with science, art, PSHE, literacy and RE. You can find ideas on the website, www.barnabasinschools.org.uk/schools6993.

*

Paul's journeys

Key Bible verse

I run towards the goal, so that I can win the prize
of being called to heaven.

PHILIPPIANS 3:14

Values

Responsibility and tolerance

This section is designed to run from after the May break until the end of the summer term. The theme is Paul's journeys and, in the big story of God's love for the world, we are remembering how Paul and others started spreading the news about Jesus. When we imagine ourselves within this part of the story, we think about what it would feel like if we joined in to do this task.

The story of the vital race is told in six parts as an illustration of the biblical account of Paul's journeys around the Mediterranean as he took the message of Jesus to the known world. This is found in the book of Acts.

- Week 1: Paul and the magician Elymas in Paphos (Acts 13:6–12)
- Week 2: Paul takes the good news to Athens (Acts 17:16–34)
- Week 3: Paul baptises in Ephesus (Acts 19:1–8)
- Week 4: Paul's speech to Agrippa (Acts 26:1–23)
- Week 5: The storm near Crete (Acts 27:13–20)
- Week 6: Paul takes the good news to Rome (Acts 28:11–16)

The storyteller's prop consists of three cuddly toys of a kind often found in charity shops.

- A big dog called Skipper
- A smaller dog called Colorado
- A small mouse called Perry

It should be possible to hold all three animals in one arm, the two dogs with an arm-hold and the mouse using a small loop of material attached to its head that can be grasped with a finger. This allows the other hand to be used to take whichever of the animals is prominent in the story at a given moment. A photograph of an example prop can be found on the website, www.barnabasinschools. org.uk/schools6993.

Suggested music

Suggestions for pre-recorded music that could be used at the start and end of the assemblies include:

- Theme tune from *Mission: Impossible* (Lalo Schifrin, Verve Records B0016453VK)
- 'Jupiter' from *The Planets Suite* (Gustav Holst, Naxos 5.110004)

Suggestions for songs that could be sung at the assemblies include:

- All over the world the Spirit is moving (JP 5)
- Colours of day (Weeks Five and Six) (JP 28)
- Do not be afraid (Week Five) (HO&N 111)
- For I'm building a people of power (JP 47)
- Lord, the light of your love is shining (SoF 362)
- One more step along the world I go (JP 188)
- You shall go out with joy (SoF 640)

The vital race: Week One

Bible link

This week's Bible passage link is Acts 13:6–12, which recounts Paul's encounter with the magician Elymas in Paphos.

Key theme

This week's key theme is 'being part of a team'. Skipper, Colorado and Perry were a team. They each had different skills, so they could help each other out and work well together. Discussion could focus around the times when people need to work together in teams, what makes a good team and the benefits of working in a team.

Episode One

Today we're starting a new story about three animals and a vital race they were running. 'Vital' means 'very important' and 'life-giving', so this story is about a race to take the gift of life to people who needed it. It's a very special story, because it tells us about God and things in the Bible.

Once upon a time, there were three animals. Their names were Skipper, Colorado and Perry. (*Show the three toy animals.*) Skipper was a strong and sturdy dog, very wise and reliable. Colorado was an inquisitive dog who always made friends with everyone she met, and Perry was a small and clever mouse who always came up with ingenious plans. They were best friends and they made a great team together. They lived in a town in

Canada, far in the north. One day, they heard about a distant village which was always in the dark, where everyone was slowly dying. The three animals were very upset by this. They wanted to do something to help.

That afternoon, the three animals were sitting by a little stream, watching the sunbeams make a pattern of bright light on the water. Suddenly Perry had an idea. 'Let's catch a little piece of this brightly lit-up water, put it into a flask and take it to the village that's in darkness. We might be able to save the people.' So he used a tiny crystal flask to catch some of the sparkling water. When he pushed the stopper in, beams of light immediately shone out everywhere. It was the brightest light the animals had ever seen! Perry quickly put the flask in a little leather bag to keep it safe and the three animals set off. It wasn't long before the road became a dusty track. On and on they went, and soon they were in the wilderness.

Just then, the three animals saw a strange-looking wolf ahead of them in the path. He had tufts of fur sticking out everywhere. 'I've not seen you before,' he said. 'Do you know about my great powers?' The three animals shook their heads. 'I can read your minds!' cried the wolf. 'Let me show you. Think of a number that's bigger than four but smaller than six.' Skipper, Colorado and Perry all thought quickly, and the wolf shouted, 'You're thinking of the number five!' Skipper and Colorado were impressed, but Perry frowned a bit and thought, 'I think this wolf is trying to trick us.'

The wolf kept on talking quickly. 'Now for something more amazing,' he said. As he spoke, Colorado noticed that lots of other wild animals were watching as well. There were beavers, badgers and a porcupine. 'I can make things disappear!' said the wolf as he put a little pebble down on the path. 'I will make this pebble vanish—but, for my power to work, you must all stare at that snowy mountain in the distance.' So the animals all concentrated on the mountain, and when they looked back the pebble had gone! Perry frowned again, but before he could say anything the wolf added, 'Now put your little leather bag down on the path and I will make it disappear as well!'

Then Perry squeaked, 'No! No! It's a trick! This wolf doesn't really have amazing powers. He's just trying to steal the flask of light!' Quick as a flash, Perry pulled the flask out of its bag. Light shone everywhere and one of the beams went straight into the eyes of the wolf. The light had blinded him and he ran off, howling. All the other wild animals started asking questions about the flask of light, so Skipper explained about their vital race to save the village that was in darkness. 'We're responsible. It's up to us,' he said.

I'll tell you more of the story about the vital race next time. It's a very special story, because it reminds us of someone who went on lots of vital journeys about 2000 years ago—a man called Paul. Paul journeyed all around the countries next to the Mediterranean Sea and, just like the animals, he was taking something vital with him—the gospel or good news of Jesus.

On the first part of his journey, Paul was at a place called Paphos. There he met a magician called Elymas, who had lots of nasty tricks, a bit like the wolf in our story. Elymas tried to oppose Paul but Paul actually made him go blind, just as the wolf was made blind. Paul told the people in Paphos about Jesus and his vital mission, just as the animals told everyone about the flask of light and their vital mission. Paul talked about being in a race. He wrote, 'I run towards the goal, so that I can

181

win the prize of being called to heaven.' It's a vital race that every Christian person is running.

I wonder what it would have been like to journey with Skipper, Colorado and Perry, taking the vital flask of light to the gloomy village. Would we have managed to scare the strange wolf away, like Perry did? And I wonder what it would have been like to have journeyed with Paul around the Mediterranean Sea, taking the good news about Jesus to places that had never heard of him. I wonder.

Suggested prayer

Lord God, the good news about Jesus gives life to those who hear it and lights up the world with your love. Help us to remember Paul, who went on a vital race to bring the message of Jesus to everyone he met. Help us to be like Paul as well, so that we too can share the good news of Jesus and reach the finishing line to be with you. Amen

The vital race: Week Two

Bible link

This week's Bible passage link is Acts 17:16–34, which recounts Paul's visit to Athens.

Key theme

This week's key theme is 'precious and valuable'. Perry knew that the most precious and valuable thing to put on the plinth was the flask of light. For many Christians, worshipping God is the most precious and valuable thing in the world. Discussion could focus around different understandings of value, what different people think is the most valuable thing in the world, and why they think so. This will also provide an opportunity to engage with the values associated with this theme, because people have a responsibility toward things that are of value and need to be tolerant of ideas that are different from their own.

Episode Two

(Show the three toy animals.) Can anyone remember the story we began last time? Who are these three animals, and what are they doing? The story reminds us about something in the Bible. Can you remember what it is?

Skipper, Colorado and Perry kept on going into the mountains. 'We're on a vital race,' Skipper reminded the other two. 'We're responsible. It's up to us.' The path went higher and higher and they started shivering in the snow. At last they reached a pass, the place where the road reached its highest point.

Blocking the pass was a huge closed gate. The three animals tried to push it open, but it wouldn't move. They tried to climb round the side, but the mountains were too steep. Then Perry noticed some writing above the gateway: 'Show me the thing of most value and I will open.' The three animals couldn't understand it, but just then a porcupine shuffled up. 'You can't get through the gate,' he said sadly. 'No one has ever got past, although hundreds have tried. It'll only open if you put the most valuable thing in the world in front of it.' The three animals were very puzzled but then Colorado said, 'Come and look!' as she pointed at five unusual statues of different things next to the pathway. The first statue was a heap of silver and gold coins. The second was some beautiful jewellery made with gems. The third was an iron crown. The fourth was a book. The fifth statue was of some little people, all kneeling down. Each of the statues had an inscription, which explained how valuable the thing was.

The animals read the inscriptions carefully. The one on the statue of the money said, 'With money you can buy anything you want.' The one with the jewellery said, 'These jewels will make you more beautiful than any other.' The one on the statue of the crown said, 'If you wear me, you will rule over others.' The one with the book said, 'In me is found all wisdom and knowledge.' Finally, the fifth inscription, on the statue of the kneeling people, said, 'These servants will do anything you wish.' 'I suppose we must choose which one is the most valuable and then place it before the gate,' said Colorado. 'They all seem very valuable.'

Perry suddenly shouted to the others, 'Look! I've found something else here on the ground, hidden in the snow.'

Quickly he uncovered it, but it looked very strange indeed. There was an inscription but there didn't seem to be a statue at all, just an empty space. The inscription said, 'An unknown statue.'

'An empty space can't be the most valuable thing,' said Skipper. 'I think it's the book.' 'Or maybe it's the beautiful jewellery,' said Colorado. Then they noticed that there were other wild animals with the porcupine—some badgers and a mountain eagle—all of them watching closely.

Perry squeaked excitedly. 'I know! We must use our precious flask of light as the last statue, the one that says "An unknown statue". The light is far more valuable than all these other things!' Before the others could stop him, Perry opened the little leather bag, placed the crystal flask full of light on top of the inscription, and carried it quickly to the gate. Immediately the gate began to open. 'That's amazing!' said the porcupine. 'I've watched hundreds of people try to get through and no one has ever succeeded. What is that light in the flask?' So Skipper started explaining to the porcupine and the other wild animals about the vital race they were on to save the village that was in darkness. 'We're responsible. It's up to us,' he said.

I'll tell you more of the story about the vital race next time. It's a very special story, because it reminds us of someone who went on lots of vital journeys about 2000 years ago—a man called Paul. Paul journeyed all around the countries next to the Mediterranean Sea and, just like the animals, he was taking something vital with him—the gospel or good news of Jesus.

On one part of his journey, Paul was in a city called Athens, where he found an altar marked, 'To an unknown god', just like the unknown statue that the animals found. Paul told the people in Athens that this unknown god was actually the Lord of heaven and earth, whose Son is Jesus, and that to know and worship him was the most precious and valuable thing in the whole world. Paul told everyone about his vital mission, just as the animals told everyone about the flask of light and their vital race. Paul talked about being in a race. He wrote, 'I run towards the goal, so that I can win the prize of being called to heaven.' It's a vital race that every Christian person is running.

I wonder what it would have been like to journey with Skipper, Colorado and Perry, taking the vital flask of light to the gloomy village. Would we have thought to use the flask of light to open the gate, like Perry did? And I wonder what it would have been like to journey with Paul around the Mediterranean Sea, taking the good news about Jesus to places that had never heard about him. I wonder.

Suggested prayer

Lord God, the good news about Jesus gives life to those who hear it and lights up the world with your love. Help us to remember Paul, who went on a vital race to bring the message of Jesus to everyone he met. Help us to be like Paul as well, so that we too can share the good news of Jesus and reach the finishing line to be with you. Amen

The vital race: Week Three

Bible link

This week's Bible passage link is Acts 19:1–8, which tells about Paul baptising new believers in Ephesus.

Key theme

This week's key theme is 'shining like a light'. People in Ephesus were baptised so that they would shine like lights in the world. Christians believe they should share the message of Jesus with other people. Discussion could focus on how each person, with their different talents, skills, interests and beliefs, can shine like a light for other people.

Episode Three

(*Show the three toy animals.*) Can anyone remember the story we're hearing? Who are these three animals and what are they doing? The story reminds us about something in the Bible. Can you remember what it is?

Skipper, Colorado and Perry were pleased to have got through the gate at the mountain pass, and they kept going quickly. The village in the north was full of people who'd never seen the light and who were slowly dying. Only the bright flask of light could help them and give them life. 'It's a vital race,' Skipper reminded the other two. 'We're responsible. It's up to us.'

The pathway led down into a valley, to a big rushing river. The animals realised they would have to cross the river. 'There's no bridge, so we'll have to make a raft using these old branches and strands of creeper,' said Perry. Before long, they'd made the raft and it floated beautifully. The bits of creeper they used to tie the branches together weren't very strong, but Perry pushed the raft off from the bank. In no time at all, they were being carried along with the flow of the water. The current was so fast that the logs started to separate. Then suddenly they rushed past some rocks and the raft broke apart completely, throwing the animals into the water. 'Swim to the bank!' shouted Skipper. They tried swimming but the current got faster than ever, pulling them along.

Then Colorado saw a massive waterfall up ahead, rushing closer and closer. Luckily, there was a rock right in the middle of the river, at the top of the waterfall. Somehow Skipper managed to grab hold of it. 'Hold on here!' he yelled above the roaring noise of the rushing water. Colorado and Perry grabbed on to him and they all stopped above the waterfall. 'We'll never survive if we go over that drop,' said Colorado, but the rock was slippery. Slowly, Skipper's paws were losing their grip and he was getting tired. All at once, he lost his grip and the three animals shot over the edge of the waterfall—down, down, down into a great big deep lake.

The lake was lovely and calm but the three animals had fallen a long way. There wasn't any sign of them for ages, but gradually they all came up to the surface again, coughing and spluttering. With difficulty, they managed to swim slowly over to the side of the lake, where there was a little beach. 'I thought I'd died!' said Perry to the others as they crawled up the sand. 'We went so deep under the water. It's almost as if we've died and then come back to life again!'

There were some friendly beavers swimming in the lake. Skipper explained about the journey the three animals were on and how they'd been carried over the waterfall. 'But why are you on this journey at all?' asked one of the beavers, so Skipper started explaining about the vital race they were on to save the village that was in darkness. 'We're responsible. It's up to us,' he said.

When Skipper was telling the beavers about the flask of light, he started to get very worried. 'Where's the flask of light?' he asked Perry. 'Is it all right after the waterfall?' Perry found the little leather bag. It was soaked, and the three animals wondered if the light would still be shining. Perry reached into the bag and pulled out the flask. Beams of light flashed out everywhere! 'It's even brighter than before!' shouted Perry joyfully. 'We can still carry on with our vital race.'

I'll tell you more of the story about the vital race next time. It's a very special story, because it reminds us of someone who went on lots of vital journeys about 2000 years ago—a man called Paul. Paul journeyed all around the countries next to the Mediterranean Sea and, just like the animals, he was taking something vital with him. He was taking the gospel or good news of Jesus.

On one part of his journey, Paul was in a place called Ephesus, where he told everyone about his vital mission, just as the animals told everyone about the flask of light. The animals were swept under water and nearly died but made a new beginning. In the same way, Paul taught everyone how water is used in baptism as a symbol to remind us how Jesus died and rose again and to help us make a new beginning in life. The flask was even brighter after being in the water, and baptism has the same effect. It helps people to shine like lights in the world. Paul talked about being in a race. He wrote, 'I run towards the goal, so that I can win the prize of being called to heaven.' It's a vital race that every Christian person is running.

But I wonder what it would have been like to journey with Skipper, Colorado and Perry, taking the vital flask of light to the gloomy village. I wonder what it would have felt like, being swept over that waterfall. And I wonder what it would have been like to journey with Paul around the Mediterranean Sea, taking the good news about Jesus to places that had never heard about him and teaching people about being baptised. I wonder.

Suggested prayer

Lord God, the good news about Jesus gives life to those who hear it and lights up the world with your love. Help us to remember Paul, who went on a vital race to bring the message of Jesus to everyone he met. Help us to be like Paul as well, so that we too can share the good news of Jesus and reach the finishing line to be with you. Amen

The vital race: Week Four

Bible link

This week's Bible passage link is Acts 26:1–23, which recounts Paul's speech to Agrippa.

Key theme

This week's key theme is 'persuasion'. The three friends in the story had to convince the chief gorilla of the value of their mission. Paul was set free because he convinced Agrippa about Jesus. Consider the power of persuasion and how it can be used for good and bad causes.

Episode Four

(Show the three toy animals.) Can anyone remember the story we're hearing? Who are these three animals, and what are they doing? The story reminds us about something in the Bible. Can you remember what it is?

Skipper, Colorado and Perry knew that they had to carry on with their journey quickly, because the village in the north was full of people who were slowly dying in darkness. Only the bright flask of light, which was safely in the little leather bag, could give them life. 'It's a vital race,' Skipper reminded the other two animals. 'We're responsible. It's up to us.'

The three animals continued along the pathway, away from the lake and into a thick forest. Strange noises came from the undergrowth. The friends grew more and more frightened, especially when they realised that glinting eyes were watching them from within the bushes. Suddenly there was a great roar and three enormous gorillas rushed out of the undergrowth. Before they could escape, Skipper, Colorado and Perry had been seized by the gorillas and tied up. Then they were carried away, through the forest.

After a long trek, the gorillas and their captives arrived at a camp in a clearing. There was a cage made of wooden logs right in the middle of the camp, and the three animals were locked inside it. 'What are we going to do now?' said Perry to the others. 'Even though I could squeeze out through one of the gaps, I don't want to carry on our journey without both of you.' The animals couldn't think what to do.

Colorado was always very friendly with everyone and soon she was talking to one of the gorilla guards. 'Gorillas don't live in Canada,' she said to the guard. 'I don't understand why you're living here in the forest.' 'We escaped from a zoo,' said the gorilla, 'and now we're in control of the whole forest. When anyone comes along the pathway, we put them in this cage.'

Several days went by before Colorado could talk to the gorilla guard again. 'If you don't help us, our vital race will fail,' she pleaded. The gorilla suddenly looked interested. 'What's this race, then?' he asked gruffly, so Skipper began to explain.

'We're on a vital race to save a whole village that is always in darkness and where the people are slowly dying. The only thing that can save them is some light, but there's no time to lose! Every day we sit here in this cage is a wasted day.' The gorilla started laughing and some others in his gang came over to the cage as well, wondering what was going on. 'Listen to the dog's crazy story,' said the gorilla, and Skipper once again explained about the village in darkness and how the people there were dying.

This time, when Skipper got to the bit about the light, Perry pulled the crystal flask out of the little leather bag. It shone brightly throughout the clearing in the forest. The gorillas were all amazed, especially their chief, who was bigger than all the others. 'What's that light in the flask?' he asked. 'This will bring life to the people who live in darkness,' said Skipper. 'We need to take it to them. We're responsible. It's up to us.' The chief gorilla looked at the flask of light again and nodded his head. 'I can see how important your vital race is. You can go free and carry on your journey.' So the guard opened the cage and Skipper, Colorado and Perry set off again, carefully carrying the precious light, which was safely packed away in its bag again.

I'll tell you more of the story about the vital race next time. It's a very special story, because it reminds us of someone who went on lots of vital journeys about 2000 years ago—a man called Paul. Paul journeyed all around the countries next to the Mediterranean Sea and, just like the animals, he was taking something vital with him—the gospel or good news of Jesus.

On one part of his journey, Paul was in a place called Caesarea, where he was arrested by some angry people, just as the animals were captured by the gorillas. Paul made a speech to a man called Agrippa in Caesarea, telling him how the good news of Jesus changed people's lives, just as the animals told the gorillas about the flask of light and their vital race. Then Agrippa let Paul go so that he could carry on his journey, just as the chief gorilla let the three animals go. In fact, Paul talked about being in a race. He wrote, 'I run towards the goal, so that

I can win the prize of being called to heaven.' It's a vital race that every Christian person is running.

I wonder what it would have been like to travel with Skipper, Colorado and Perry, taking the vital flask of light to the gloomy village. I wonder what it was like to be captured by the gorillas and shut in the cage. It must have felt amazing when the chief gorilla saw the light and let them go. And I wonder what it would have been like to journey with Paul around the Mediterranean Sea, taking the good news about Jesus to places that had never heard about him. I wonder.

Suggested prayer

Lord God, the good news about Jesus gives life to those who hear it and lights up the world with your love. Help us to remember Paul, who went on a vital race to bring the message of Jesus to everyone he met. Help us to be like Paul as well, so that we too can share the good news of Jesus and reach the finishing line to be with you. Amen

The vital race: Week Five

Bible link

This week's Bible passage link is Acts 27:13–20, which tells how Paul was caught up in a storm near Crete.

Key theme

This week's key theme is 'fear'. The bears and the three friends were afraid in the storm. When people are afraid, they cannot always think straight and don't know what to do. Sometimes people need help to overcome their fears. The storm did not go away but the light helped all the animals to feel less afraid. Discussion might focus on examples of times when people have been afraid and things that have helped them overcome their fears. Consideration might be given to the idea that sometimes we are afraid of things we don't understand properly. For example, before they were understood, solar eclipses terrified people, and people who thought the world was flat were afraid they might fall off the edge.

Episode Five

(Show the three toy animals.) Can anyone remember the story we're hearing? Who are these three animals, and what are they doing? The story reminds us about something in the Bible. Can you remember what it is?

Skipper, Colorado and Perry quickly hurried down the path that the gorilla chief had shown them. They were pleased to be free again but they were worried about the village far to the north, where the people had never seen any light and were slowly dying. Only the bright flask of light could help them. 'It's a vital race,' Skipper reminded the other two animals. 'We're responsible. It's up to us.'

The pathway led out of the forest and into a valley with steep slopes and a river. Before long, the river flowed into a huge lake, which stretched as far as the eye could see. 'What do we do now?' Colorado asked the others. 'The path has come to an end.' Perry peered out across the lake. 'Everything is very dark but I think the village we're looking for is over there on the other side.' Skipper and Colorado couldn't see that far but they knew that Perry's eyes were very sharp. 'How can we possibly cross over such a big lake?' wondered Skipper.

Just then, they noticed a big eagle perched nearby and Colorado ran over to say hello. She started to explain about the vital race. 'We've got to get the light over to that village. Can you help us?' 'I could fly you over the lake,' answered the eagle, 'but I don't want to carry that flask of light. It makes me nervous.' Skipper, Colorado and Perry knew it wouldn't be any good just talking to the people in the village about the light— they had to take the light itself. So they thanked the eagle, but said that they didn't need his help.

Colorado noticed another creature near the lake. She ran over and discovered that it was a giant mole. She started to explain to the mole about the vital race they were running. 'We've got to get the light over to that village. Maybe you could dig a deep tunnel under the lake for us?' The mole smiled and answered, 'I dig the best tunnels in the world, but not even I can dig a tunnel under the lake. I could dig one through this steep hill for you, instead.' Skipper, Colorado and Perry shook their heads. They had to go to the village—nowhere else would do. So they thanked the mole, but said that they didn't need his help.

Suddenly Colorado was running off again. She'd seen a boat down at the edge of the water, with a crew of brown bears. Colorado explained to them about the vital race. 'We've got to get the light over to that village. We're responsible. It's up to us. Can you take us in your boat?' The bears looked at one another and their captain said, 'We could take you over, but the lake gets very rough and dangerous. It might be the last journey you ever make. Are you sure you want to go?' Skipper, Colorado and Perry knew that this was their only chance to cross over to the village. 'Yes, take us over the lake, please,' they answered as they got on board.

The boat set sail but soon the wind blew stronger and the waves grew higher. The sky turned completely black and even the bears began to look frightened. 'Throw everything overboard!' shouted the bear captain. 'We must save the ship!' So the bears started throwing some of the cargo overboard. It felt as though the ship would sink at any minute, and it was so dark that everyone was terrified. But then Perry had a really good idea.

I haven't got time to tell you any more of the story today, but I'll carry on next time. As you know, it's a very special story. It reminds us of someone who went on lots of vital journeys about 2000 years ago—a man called Paul. Paul journeyed all around the countries next to the Mediterranean Sea and, just like the animals, he was taking something vital with him—the gospel or good news of Jesus.

On one part of his journey, Paul took a ship in the Mediterranean and he sailed past an island called Crete. There was a great storm and the sky turned black, just like in our story when the storm hit the lake. Everyone on the ship with Paul was terrified but he had an idea. I wonder if you can guess what he did, especially if you can remember what he wrote. Paul talked about being in a race. He wrote, 'I run towards the goal, so that I can win the prize of being called to heaven.' It's a vital race that every Christian person is running.

I wonder what it would have been like to journey with Skipper, Colorado and Perry, taking the vital flask of light to the gloomy village. I wonder if we would have been brave enough to go on the ship, even though it was very dangerous. And I wonder what it would have been like to journey with Paul around the Mediterranean Sea, taking the good news about Jesus to places that had never heard about him. I wonder.

Suggested prayer

Lord God, the good news about Jesus gives life to those who hear it and lights up the world with your love. Help us to remember Paul, who went on a vital race to bring the message of Jesus to everyone he met. Help us to be like Paul as well, so that we too can share the good news of Jesus and reach the finishing line to be with you. Amen

The vital race: Week Six

Bible link

This week's Bible passage link is Acts 28:11–16, which recounts Paul's arrival in Rome.

Key theme

This week's key theme is 'making a difference'. The arrival of the light in the village saved lives, and Christians believe that the good news about Jesus changes people's lives. Lots of people do jobs that make a big difference to the lives of others—for example, doctors, nurses, fire fighters and teachers. However, all these people can only really make a difference if the people they are trying to help accept the help that is offered. This balance engages well with the value of responsibility. Discussion could focus on classroom or school examples, as well as examples of people who are advised by doctors to exercise or not to smoke, but choose not to follow the advice.

Episode Six

(*Show the three toy animals.*) Can anyone remember the story we're hearing? Who are these three animals, and what are they doing? The story reminds us about something in the Bible. Can you remember what it is?

The storm on the lake and the dark sky made everyone in the boat terrified, but then Perry had a really good idea. He found the little leather bag and carefully pulled out the crystal flask. Bright beams of light suddenly shone everywhere and Perry shouted out as loudly as he could, 'Don't be afraid! We'll be safe with this light to help us.'

The captain of the bears clambered over to have a closer look at the light in the flask, and Skipper started explaining about the vital race they were on to save the village that was in darkness. He explained how they'd trapped some light in the flask to start with, and how they'd met the wolf who'd tried to trick them. Then Skipper described the mountain pass and the mysterious gate, which opened when the light was put in front of it. Then he told how they'd survived the waterfall and how the light had become even brighter. Then he explained about the gorillas in the jungle, who'd shut them in a cage, and about how they'd reached the lake. 'We're responsible. It's up to us,' he said. 'We've got to take this flask of light to the village that's in darkness. Nothing else will save the people there.'

By now the wind had dropped, but it was still very dark as they reached the shore. 'I don't know how anyone could live here,' whispered Colorado to the others. 'No wonder the village is slowly dying.' The three animals ran up the path into the village and held the light up high. 'We've brought you the gift of light,' shouted Perry, and slowly the villagers came out of their houses to see what all the fuss was about. They were very ill and weak and they shielded their eyes from the light.

Skipper, Colorado and Perry knew that this was the chance for the people to live—but then a very sad thing happened. Some of the villagers covered up their eyes with their hands and started grumbling. 'We don't want this light!' they said. 'We're quite happy the way we are. Leave us alone!' 'But you're dying,' said Colorado to them. 'This light will help you to recover and live!' But the villagers ignored her and stumbled back into their houses, getting weaker with each step they took. Colorado had tears in her eyes. 'After all those journeys we made and all the risks we took, they didn't even want this precious gift,' she sobbed.

But Perry noticed that a few of the villagers were still out on the path, peering at the light. They were creeping closer, with smiles on their faces. One of them said, 'I feel stronger and happier already! The light is bringing me back to life. Thank you for this special gift—but I know another village even further to the north, which is in darkness as well. Can I take the flask to them, to save them too?' 'Yes, of course you can,' Perry said with delight. 'We want everyone in the whole world to have a chance of being saved by the light.' The three animals looked at each other. They knew that their vital race was over and they'd made it to the finishing line, but they knew that others would continue the race as well.

That's almost the end of our story about the vital race. It's a very special story, because it reminds us of someone who went on lots of vital journeys about 2000 years ago—a man called Paul. Paul journeyed all around the countries next to the Mediterranean Sea and, just like the animals, he was taking something vital with him—the gospel or good news of Jesus.

In the end, Paul reached the place he was heading for, a great big city called Rome. When he got there, he told everyone about Jesus, who gives the gift of true life to all who accept him. But some people didn't want to hear, just like the villagers in our story who crept away. Luckily, some people did listen to Paul and they accepted the message about Jesus. They even wanted to spread the good news themselves, just like the villager who wanted to take the flask of light and continue the vital race. In fact, Paul talked about being in a race. He wrote, 'I run towards the goal, so that I can win the prize of being called to heaven.' It's a vital race that every Christian person is running.

I wonder what it would have been like to travel with Skipper, Colorado and Perry, taking the vital flask of light to the gloomy village on that vital race. How would we have felt when some of the villagers didn't want to see the light after all? How would we have felt when someone actually wanted to carry on the race, to try to save another village? And I wonder what it would have been like to journey with Paul around the Mediterranean Sea and to Rome, taking the good news about Jesus to places that had never heard about him. I wonder.

Suggested prayer

Lord God, the good news about Jesus gives life to those who hear it and lights up the world with your love. Help us to remember Paul, who went on a vital race to bring the message of Jesus to everyone he met. Help us to be like Paul as well, so that we too can share the good news of Jesus and reach the finishing line to be with you. Amen

The vital race: Concluding celebration

The story of the vital race is designed to end with a leavers' service or celebration, using suitable songs and readings. The concluding episode reminds us that as we move on through life, we can change the lives of others. Our lives are like a story and we can become part of God's story if we choose to do so. The six different stories from the year join together into one big story and, as we become familiar with this story, our lives are enriched.

Concluding episode

Do you remember the story of the vital race and the three animals who had to make that long journey? *(Show the three toy animals.)* Who can remember their names? Who can remember the adventures they had as they carried the flask of light safely in its little leather bag? And when Skipper, Colorado and Perry finally arrived in the village, who can remember what happened then?

The journey made by the three animals reminds us of the journeys made by Paul, which we can read about in the Bible. When the animals arrived at the village, they wondered if the flask of light had finished its journey, but some of the people there wanted to share the light with other villages. The vital race kept on going. It was the same for Paul. He took the message about Jesus to everyone he met and then some of those people shared it with others. Soon the good news about Jesus had spread more and more. That good news goes around the world when people hear about Jesus and decide to tell other people, too.

Each of the stories we've heard this year is part of one big story. All of those stories remind us of things in the Bible and, for Christians, the Bible tells God's story.

(*Show the pole and ribbons from the story of Felix's garden.*) Do you remember these ribbons? Whose garden do they come from? Felix made a beautiful garden but it was ruined by the little robin. Even though there was a new beginning, the birds never learnt to look after the garden properly. The story of Felix's garden reminded us of something in the Bible. God's creation is beautiful but human beings don't look after it properly. God needed to send some special help.

(*Show the candles from the story of the candle-maker.*) Do you remember these candles? Who made them? The candle-maker was hoping that each candle would be the best one ever made, but none of them was. She waited for a long time and, in the end, the greatest candle of all did appear. The story of the candle-maker reminded us of something in the Bible. The prophets waited for ages, because they knew that someone greater than all of them would appear in the end. That person was Jesus.

(*Show the crown and jewels from the story of Cassandra's crown.*) Do you remember this crown? Who wore it? Cassandra went on an amazing adventure to discover the secret of the crown, and these five jewels appeared one by one. The story of Cassandra's crown reminded us of something in the Bible. Jesus told many different parables but they all explained what it's like to live in his kingdom. Although it's like a secret, everyone can discover it for themselves.

(*Show the perch with the five birds from the story of the witness birds.*) Do you remember these birds? What was special about them? They witnessed many different things in history, but the thing they remembered most of all was the day when Jesus died, which is recorded in the Bible. *(Remove the birds and turn the perch into the cross with nails.)* The birds thought Jesus had made a big mistake, but in fact his humility gave hope to the world. *(Turn the cross round to show the message 'He is risen'.)*

(Show the flowerpot and flowers from the story of the amazing flowerpot.) Do you remember who grew these amazing flowers? Percy was worried when the seeds seemed to die, but on the third day they came to life. To start with, he wasn't sure the flowers were real, but he could smell, taste, see, touch and hear them. The last flower was so high that Percy knew it must be able to watch over everything. The story of the amazing flowerpot reminded us of something in the Bible. Jesus died but on the third day he rose again. Although we can't see him now, Christians believe he is watching over everything still.

(Show the three animals from the story of the vital race.) Skipper, Colorado and Perry took the flask of light to people who were living in darkness. The story of the vital race reminded us of something in the Bible, just like all the other stories. Paul shared the good news about Jesus with everyone.

All these stories are part of one big story. It's God's story. It's the story we must keep on telling and sharing with everyone, just as Skipper, Colorado and Perry shared the flask of light. The amazing thing is that we can be part of that story as well. When we play our part in God's story, we'll find ourselves blessed by him.

Today we're praying especially for our leavers. Some of you have been at this school for six years and now you're leaving. You're on a journey and God will be with you. Even if we're not leaving this year, though, we're still on a journey through life. All of us are journeying with God as we live our lives. We're in God's great big story. Do you remember what Paul wrote? Paul talked about being in a race. The words he wrote are in the Bible. 'I run towards the goal, so that I can win the prize of being called to heaven.' It's the vital race that every Christian person is running in the journey through life.

*

The vital race:
Ideas for classroom follow up

Alongside the main weekly assembly, you can develop the themes of the story in your classroom. One or more of the following ideas could be used.

- The biblical narratives about Paul's journeys can be explored fully and in detail using the references on page 177. Drama strategies could be used to encourage pupils to engage with the stories. There is much more about Paul, his faith and his journeys that could be explored. The Culham website has four short PowerPoint presentations about him: www.cowo.culham. ac.uk/reflections/061p_paul.php
- Explore the values related to this term's theme—responsibility and tolerance.
- Consider other examples of the sort of determination shown by the three friends (for example, Mary Jones or Gladys Aylward) and explore the relevance and value of determination in the lives and work of pupils.
- Explore examples of people who have helped others; famous and local examples can be used.

There are possible curriculum links with PE, science, literacy, PSHE, Citizenship, geography and RE. You can find ideas on the website, www.barnabasinschools.org.uk/schools6993.

*

Templates

God's storyteller badge

The witness birds: Sparrow

The witness birds: Dove

The witness birds: Owl

The witness birds: Cockerel

The witness birds: Crow

The witness birds

To make the perch and cross

You will need:

- A 2m plank with cross-section 70mm by 8mm ideally (or something similar), to make two lengths of wood, one 60cm and the other 120cm.
- 4cm nails, with a substantial head.
- Any suitable nut and bolt with a metal washer to make the pivot.
- Red paint for the words on the reverse.

1. Cut the two pieces of wood from the plank and smooth with sandpaper.
2. Drill a hole in each piece of wood, 44cm along the longer piece and centrally in the shorter piece. Use the nut, bolt and washer to create a pivot using the holes in the planks (the head of the bolt can be covered with filler to camouflage it).
3. Hammer the five nails into the planks at the points identified in the diagram opposite. The first nail is about 2cm in from the end (the nails can be slightly off-centre to keep them in a line, avoiding the pivot).
4. Paint in red the words 'He is alive' on the reverse of the smaller piece of wood so that when the cross is turned round, the message shows (the words are hidden when in the perch configuration).
5. The nut should be tightened so that the two pieces of wood are held securely in place, but so that it is possible to swing the crosspiece out fairly easily. The nails are at 21cm intervals to allow the A4 pictures to be hung alongside one another.

Perch configuration

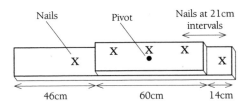

Nails

Pivot

Nails at 21cm intervals

46cm   60cm   14cm

Cross configuration

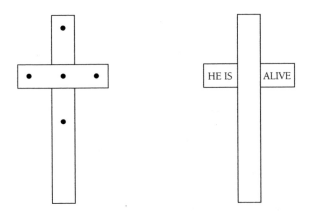

HE IS   ALIVE

*

Bible index

Old Testament

*

Index of values and key themes

Values

Key themes

Also from BRF/Barnabas

More Collective Worship Unwrapped

20 tried and tested story-based assemblies for primary schools

John Guest

More Collective Worship Unwrapped is a flexible and practical resource ideal for all teachers seeking to grasp the key principles of collective worship as quickly and as effectively as possible. The material is equally valuable for both experienced and newly qualified teachers, as well as RE coordinators and those invited into schools to lead collective worship.

Following the success of *Collective Worship Unwrapped*, this second book provides a further 20 story-based assemblies to use with Key Stages One and Two. As before, each of the assemblies gives a Bible base, tips on presentation, visual aids required, recommended songs, an optional prayer and follow-up material.

Once again, the stories have all been written for live situations. Their inspiration has come from many sources but, above all, each one is based on and inspired by stories from the Bible. Each outline can be set in the context of a variety of topical themes, including moral and personal development, citizenship, spiritual values, seasons of the Christian year and special times.

ISBN 978 1 84101 664 1   £12.99
To order a copy of this book, use the order form on page 227 or visit www.brfonline.org.uk.

Assemblies for Autumn Festivals
27 ready-to-use ideas for festivals and feast days

Martin Cox

This book is packed with 27 tried-and-tested assembly ideas designed to resource both popular and lesser-known festivals in the first term of the new school year. The ideas fall under four main themes—Harvest, Saints, Remembrance and Advent—with at least two assemblies to choose from within each theme.

The material is flexible in that the assemblies can be used with a 'dip in and try' approach, followed in date order, or used to explore one of the four key themes. Topics covered include Harvest, St Matthew, Michaelmas, St Francis, St Luke, All Saints, Guy Fawkes, Remembrance, Christ the King, St Andrew, St Nicholas and Advent.

Each assembly includes key background information for the teacher, Bible links, creative ideas for introducing the theme, suggestions for visual aids and ideas for exploring the theme, including storytelling drama, music, songs and prayers. Also, each assembly is backed up by a wealth of ideas for cross-curricular extension work in the classroom.

ISBN 978 1 84101 459 3   £7.99
To order a copy of this book, use the order form on page 227 or visit www.brfonline.org.uk.

Eyewitness Assemblies

15 ready-to-use assemblies for Easter to Pentecost

Gaynor Cobb

From Palm Sunday to Pentecost, *Eyewitness Assemblies* presents 15 short stories giving imaginative 'first hand' accounts told from the perspective of a character in the original Bible story. The eyewitness account is followed by a reflective poem, role-play or news report to help spark children's imaginations and enable them to get under the skin of the story. Each unit is stand-alone, while at the same time giving a clear and comprehensive picture of the part of the Christian story that led to Jesus' death and resurrection and the birth of the early Church.

The material is ideal for Key Stage 2, and class or whole-school assemblies, over the Easter period, or in RE at other times of year. Overall notes give general PSHE/Citizenship and RE links so that the assemblies could be followed up in class. This may be of particular use where the assembly forms part of the RE syllabus. There is also a helpful glossary and Bible index.

ISBN 978 1 84101 496 8   £7.99

To order a copy of this book, use the order form on page 227 or visit www.brfonline.org.uk.

Stories for Interactive Assemblies

15 story-based assemblies to get children talking

Nigel Bishop

Collective worship is an ideal time to combine biblical teaching with contemporary storytelling. The 15 easy-to-tell, contemporary stories in this book are all based in the world of the classroom but have their roots in the parables of Jesus. They are designed to stimulate children's thinking and get them talking in the assembly and afterwards in the classroom.

As a means of teaching, the parables are vivid, challenging and memorable. They have been described as 'earthly stories with a heavenly meaning'. Primary children of all ages will recognise themselves and their classmates in the stories and, even if they do not recognise the original story, they are invited to relate to the underlying message that is the essence of the parable.

Each story is followed by questions for the assembly or classroom, designed to help the children interact with some of the issues raised, plus suggestions for practical activities, based on different learning styles.

ISBN 978 1 84101 465 4   £6.99

To order a copy of this book, use the order form on page 227 or visit www.brfonline.org.uk.

ORDERFORM

REF	TITLE	PRICE	QTY	TOTAL
664 1	More Collective Worship	£12.99		
459 3	Assemblies for Autumn Festivals	£7.99		
496 8	Eyewitness Assemblies	£7.99		
465 4	Stories for Interactive Assemblies	£6.99		

POSTAGE AND PACKING CHARGES				
Order value	UK	Europe	Surface	Air Mail
£7.00 & under	£1.25	£3.00	£3.50	£5.50
£7.10–£30.00	£2.25	£5.50	£6.50	£10.00
Over £30.00	FREE	prices on request		

Postage and packing	
Donation	
TOTAL	

Name _____ Account Number _____

Address _____

_____ Postcode _____

Telephone Number_____

Email _____

Payment by: ❑ Cheque ❑ Mastercard ❑ Visa ❑ Postal Order ❑ Maestro

Card no ☐☐☐☐ ☐☐☐☐ ☐☐☐☐ ☐☐☐☐ ☐☐☐

Valid from ☐☐☐☐ Expires ☐☐☐☐ Issue no. ☐☐☐

Security code* ☐☐☐ *Last 3 digits on the reverse of the card.
ESSENTIAL IN ORDER TO PROCESS YOUR ORDER

Shaded boxes for Maestro use only

Signature _____ Date _____

All orders must be accompanied by the appropriate payment.

Please send your completed order form to:
BRF, 15 The Chambers, Vineyard, Abingdon OX14 3FE
Tel. 01865 319700 / Fax. 01865 319701 Email: enquiries@brf.org.uk

❑ Please send me further information about BRF publications.

Available from your local Christian bookshop.   BRF is a Registered Charity

❧ barnabas

Resourcing **Collective Worship and Assemblies, RE, Festivals, Drama** and **Art** in primary schools

- Barnabas RE Days—exploring Christianity creatively
- INSET
- Books and resources
- www.barnabasinschools.org.uk